Oneida (Community) Limited

A Goodly Heritage Gone Wrong

John P. L. Hatcher

iUniverse

ONEIDA (COMMUNITY) LIMITED
A GOODLY HERITAGE GONE WRONG

Copyright © 2016 J.P.L. Hatcher.

All rights reserved. No part of this book may be used or reproduced by any means, graphic, electronic, or mechanical, including photocopying, recording, taping or by any information storage retrieval system without the written permission of the author except in the case of brief quotations embodied in critical articles and reviews.

iUniverse books may be ordered through booksellers or by contacting:

iUniverse
1663 Liberty Drive
Bloomington, IN 47403
www.iuniverse.com
1-800-Authors (1-800-288-4677)

Because of the dynamic nature of the Internet, any web addresses or links contained in this book may have changed since publication and may no longer be valid. The views expressed in this work are solely those of the author and do not necessarily reflect the views of the publisher, and the publisher hereby disclaims any responsibility for them.

Any people depicted in stock imagery provided by Thinkstock are models, and such images are being used for illustrative purposes only. Certain stock imagery © Thinkstock.

ISBN: 978-1-5320-0296-0 (sc)
ISBN: 978-1-5320-0297-7 (hc)
ISBN: 978-1-5320-0334-9 (e)

Library of Congress Control Number: 2016911925

Print information available on the last page.

iUniverse rev. date: 09/30/2016

Dedication

To the generations of Oneida Ltd. employees who
built and preserved for over one hundred years
both a "Goodly Heritage"
and
"A company different from any company you have ever heard of"

Contents

Preface ix
Introduction xv

1 Pierrepont B. Noyes, 1897-1950 1
2 Miles E. Robertson, 1926-1959 13
3 Stainless Steel 25
4 Pierrepont T. Noyes, 1960-1981 33
5 John L. Marcellus, 1981-1986 47
6 William D. Matthews, 1986-1999 55
7 Peter J. Kallet, 1999-2006 71
8 Epilogue: Bankruptcy and Beyond 97

Addendums
    Appendix 1   The Need for Diversification 107
    Appendix 2   Company Parts 115
    Appendix 3   Money Spent vs. Money Earned 118
    Appendix 4   Corporate Financial Highlights 119
    Appendix 5   Special Benefits and Contracts 120
    Appendix 6   Presidential Salary Growth 121
    Appendix 7   GNP vs Corporate Profit Graph 122

Acknowledgements 123

With its GOODLY HERITAGE of more than one hundred successful years of existence, ONEIDA LTD. is dedicated to making the Corporation a continuously profitable venture, thus providing its owners with security and growth, and its members with an opportunity to earn a good living under fine working conditions.

The Oneida Ltd. Creed

We believe that the business of the Corporation must be conducted in every respect so that the shareholders' investment will be safe and will earn an adequate return. *We believe* that the policies governing our employee relations must be such that our members know that the profits from their labors are shared with them. *We believe* that we must pay wages and benefits which will not only attract the best talent for all positions, but will lead the individual to give more of himself than he would elsewhere because he knows that he is being treated fairly and will have a more fruitful and happy life with this Company. *We believe* that in all our dealings with stockholders, employees, customers, suppliers and financial institutions we must be scrupulously honest and fair. *We believe* that our products must be the best that we know how to produce... which means the best value in the market. *We believe* that we must justify our reputation as a professionally managed business, which means that our future will unfold by design rather than by chance; that our present and prospective managers will be initially and continually trained in the principles, skills, tools, ethics and disciplines of management. *We believe* that, as an organization and as individuals, we must be good citizens in our community.

We firmly believe in the "FAMILY SPIRIT" way of operating because it, by definition, implies cooperation and teamwork. This belief in the ONEIDA LTD. family makes for a strong, self-perpetuating organization which receives its strength from a *united endeavor*.

January 1, 1967 —P. T. NOYES, *President*

Preface

Anthony Wonderley
Curator of Collections and Interpretation
Oneida Community Mansion House

This book provides the last chapter of a wonderful American story that began in the mid 1800's with a famous utopia, a program for harmonious group living. The Oneida Community continued through the 1900s as a manufacturing company (Oneida Community, Ltd.) that became the largest maker of tableware in the world. The story ends in failure and failed management during the early 2000s, sad events detailed here for the first time.

Located in central upstate New York, the Oneida Community was a commune of about 250 souls dedicated to living selflessly together as one family (1848-80). Its central utopian principal was that, if men and women mingled together in all daily activities, life would be enjoyable and labor fun.

The Oneida Community was also a religious sect forged in red-hot waves of Protestant revivals scorching the countryside around 1830 and spawning new religions such as Oneida's Perfectionism. The core idea of the new faith was that, given the Christian promise of salvation from sin and given the belief that Christ had redeemed that promise, the true believer becoming one with Christ was freed from sin. In a religious sense, to be without sin is to be perfect. Those who accepted this doctrine were called Perfectionists.

The same climate of religious enthusiasm encouraged the belief that Christ was about to return bringing with him the Kingdom of Heaven—that is, the Millennium was nigh. Sharing this belief, the Perfectionists of Oneida were dedicated to bringing heaven to earth.

Oneida's founder and leader was John Humphrey Noyes—utopian scholar, Perfectionist, and a believer in Christ's imminent return. Noyes thought he could prepare the world for Christ's rule and help to bring it about with a two-part plan.

First, he would form a fellowship of believers who would imitate life in heaven, a place they imagined to be occupied by one big family sharing everything. This was called Bible communism. The term derived not from Marx, Lenin, or Mao but from the description of Epiphany given in the New Testament. Second, the fellowship would counteract sin by practicing its opposite. To the Oneida Community, sin was selfishness. Therefore, their goal was to be selfless in every act.

The Oneida Perfectionists were New Englanders, many with strong abolitionist leanings. However, the form of bondage that most bothered them was the state of a married woman who, in their time and place, had few legal, political, or reproductive rights. The Oneidans' response to this injustice was that, in their system, all adult men and women were heterosexual spouses to one another. That kind of non-exclusive and non-possessive matrimony seemed to them more just than any monogamous marriage in the larger society. Not surprisingly, Oneida was notorious in the outside world for free love. Within the commune, however, the Perfectionists were logically following out a program to share everything and to act selflessly.

If Oneida was notable for love, it was even more remarkable for its industrial success. The economy of the commune was based, not on agriculture or on small-scale craft production, but on factory manufacture. Oneida became the largest maker of metal animal traps in the U. S. and one of the country's leading producers of sewing machine thread. Traps and thread placed Oneida in the mainstream of American industrial development. The Community, as a result, took on a real industrial character.

Industrial output was based on employing outside workers to run machines. "Hirelings," however, raised a moral dilemma because wage labor, as the communards of Oneida saw it, was only slightly better than slave labor. As people who led deeply self-examined lives, the Perfectionists wondered whether being employers could be reconciled with their communal, selfless values. The ethics of this issue bothered them and they never resolved it

They did, however, answer it in a practical way. Their working solution was to be good to their employees. Assuming some responsibility for worker well-being, the Perfectionists formulated a generous personnel policy which featured good wages and decent working conditions. The Community offered a wide range of education and transportation benefits. The Perfectionists feasted their employees with strawberries and fêted them with music. By the 1870s, employees were also provided with shelter. The Perfectionists were, in their time, exceptionally good employers.

In the face of hostility emanating from Victorian prudery, the Perfectionists voluntarily disbanded the commune. By vote (199 to 1), the Oneida Community transformed itself into a business, a company called Oneida Community, Ltd. on January 1, 1881. Former members of the Oneida Community became stockholders in a company that was supposed to continue the successful industries of the Oneida Community. The company was also supposed to take care of the communal home, the Mansion House.

The company barely survived its first years under aging communists and spiritualists. It was saved by the return of the Oneida Community's now-grown children led by Pierrepont Noyes. The younger generation refocused the firm on high-end silverware. Their success was such, as you will learn in this book, that the Oneida Community. Ltd. became renowned for quality silverware and effective advertising.

At the same moment the young people committed the company to silverware, they embarked on an ambitious and risky program of welfare capitalism—the employer's assumption of responsibility for the well-being of employees. At its center was the creation of an independent workers' community, the City of Sherrill built on what was formerly Oneida Community farmland. At a time of little governmental interest in the laboring class, the Oneida company contributed substantially to Sherrill in order to ensure that a high standard of living obtained there.

To encourage private home ownership, for example, the company sold lots to its employees below market value and then gave them cash bonuses to build houses. The firm funded electrical, water, and sewage systems; fire protection and garbage collection; and facilities for public health and recreation. To encourage quality education, the Oneida Community, Ltd. donated lots for schools and contributed more than half the cost of erecting the buildings. The company assumed half the salary paid to each teacher from city tax money, then, for a dollar, made every teacher eligible for all company benefits. Teachers could live, free room and board, in the company's central building.

What the younger people did was to redefine the old Oneida Community family so that it was now the entire company. Furthermore, it was affirmed that everyone sharing in production was entitled to share in the benefits of production. Company officials said this was not philanthropy; it was just good business. As an enterprise devoted to employee welfare, Sherrill was one of the great successes in American business. To many, it was like a second utopia—one coming directly out of the people and values of the Oneida Community.

If you had grown up in Kenwood, the neighborhood around the Mansion House, before, say, 1950, you would be familiar with the history of industrial success from the Oneida Community to Oneida Ltd. (the company name after 1935). In all likelihood, you would be proud that the history also was one of continuous idealism. Both the Oneida commune and the Oneida company made money but both tried to better the world. For the Oneida Community, neglecting the welfare of others was regarded as sinful. For the Oneida company, doing well in business required doing good by the employees. Both were parts of the same century-long narrative about generous people.

The people around you in Kenwood would be associated with the company. Many of your friends would expect to be working for the company. Oneida history and values would be in the air you breathed. They would also be in your blood if you happened to be the great-grandson of John Humphrey Noyes, the grandson of Pierrepont Noyes, and nephew of Pete Noyes (president of Oneida Ltd. after 1960)—the person known formally as John Pierrepont Langford Hatcher, author of the book. You can see why he is commonly called "Lang".

Lang graduated from nearby Colgate University in 1954 at age 21. After two years of military service, he attended the Wharton School of Finance and Commerce (University of Pennsylvania), emerging with an MBA in 1958. The Wharton background helps to explain the perspective of this book. A strength of this account of the company story is employing financial analysis to clarify Oneida Ltd.'s denouement.

It was something of a tradition among Oneida Community descendants to begin one's business career elsewhere so that one returned to Oneida seasoned with outside experience. So it happened to Lang who started out as an account executive at the McCann-Erikson Advertising Agency of New York City.

The early part of Lang's Oneida career (begun 1961) was spent at the company's subsidiary in Northern Ireland. Over the course of eight years there, he rose from advertising and merchandising manager, to sales director, to managing director—head of UK operations. Back at corporate headquarters in 1970, he was placed in charge of Oneida Ltd.'s program of long-range planning. In that capacity, he pushed strongly for diversification. In 1973, he was appointed to the firm's Board of Directors. Several years later he was appointed Director of North American Subsidiaries which meant overseeing three companies including Camden Wire described in some detail in this book.

What Lang directed was profitable. UK sales increased several hundred per cent under his supervision and a ten percent bottom line for the affiliation was achieved. The companies he was later put in charge of came to produce over half of Oneida's operating profits.

But Lang and many other company employees felt increasingly out of step with Oneida Ltd. management culture as it developed in the 1980's after Pete Noyes retired. As you will learn in this book, things changed. As those at the top moved away from the tradition of Pierrepont Noyes and Dunc Robertson, the atmosphere turned distinctly chilly for Oneida Community descendants. Lang describes a board meeting (1977, Chapter 4) at which a number of internal people were demoted. He was one of them. Lang was not fired as were many other descendants, especially during the early 1980s, but he was peripheralized

Lang retired from the company in 1995. At that point Lang and his lovely wife, Nini (another descendant from another family of Oneida Ltd. officials), had raised four children and might reasonably look forward to some quality down time in their Kenwood home, a house next door to the Sales Office (the administrative building of Oneida Ltd.).

Looking out his window, Lang literally, over the next few years, saw Oneida Ltd. plummet into bankruptcy. He followed its fortunes; kept in touch with company friends; studied the company literature; pored over newspaper accounts of the debacle.

Trying to understand what happened, he wrote this book. It is something of a history and an elegy to the first company leaders. In addition to providing historical background, it charts the company's economic ups and downs in the manner of an annual report. It is a discursive financial balance sheet leading up to an analysis of the collapse. It is, finally, a memoir of Oneida Ltd., an anecdotal, first-hand picture of top company executives.

One thing not in this book that the reader should know is this. During the late 1970s and early 1980s, Oneida Community descendants became worried about the future of the Mansion House at roughly the same time as Oneida Ltd sought to divest the Mansion House. A group was organized to separate the two with the hope that an independent Mansion House might survive. As a result, the stately residence of the Oneida Community became a not-for-profit museum called the Oneida Community Mansion House. Lang played a prominent role in that development. He helped to create the new organization, then guided it through its first difficult decade (1989-99). He remains active today on a committee charged with oversight of the museum's preservation policy.

Lang's book closes in meditation on a work of textile art by Jessie Kinsley, artist of the Oneida Community, then hanging in the board room of the Sales Office. That braided tapestry, *Memory Hither Come*, presided over every important decision of the company for nearly a century. Lang had the foresight in 2007 to buy the composition—from Oneida Ltd. for the Mansion House—with the understanding that it would stay in place until the company was gone. In 2014, *Memory* was transferred to the Mansion House where it began a new watch over Oneida tradition. The owner of the tapestry at that point was EveryWare Global, Inc., which then donated a treasure trove of Oneida Ltd. materials to the Mansion House for safekeeping in perpetuity. It was a *beau geste*, an act of generosity greatly appreciated by the recipients.

I am proud to know Lang Hatcher and recommend his book to you.

Introduction

The Oneida Community founded in 1848 was a utopian society based on a belief in "Perfectionism" as practiced and promoted by its leader and my great grandfather, John Humphrey Noyes. He sought to create a society in which there would be no need to sin since all things—women and men included—were held in common. Thus, would "perfection" be achieved, both individually and collectively.

For the first few years of its existence, the community paid its bills and avoided starvation thanks to capital provided by new members who turned in their assets upon joining. There was obviously a limit for this type of financing and various commercial activities were begun to provide income—farming, canning of fruits and vegetables, luggage manufacture, silk thread refining and, penultimately, the manufacture of the product that was the community's economic salvation—animal traps.

A local trapper and blacksmith had joined the community and he happened to have invented an animal trap that was superior to anything on the market in terms of effectiveness and reliability. Being pacifists and permitting no weapons, the members were somewhat reluctant to make a product that brought distress and death to its victims. However, the community was a lot more reluctant to starve. These traps were soon sold throughout the United States and, eventually, the world.

Although community membership reached over 300 people at one point, outside labor had to be taken on to man their various workshops. The community had always been considered a good neighbor and now it was recognized as a fair and honest employer concerned for the welfare of its employees. This concern would always be the case with the Oneida Community and its eventual successor, Oneida Ltd.

The ultimate product produced by the community was table flatware. This resulted from the proximity of Oneida's branch community in

Wallingford, Ct., to the Meridan Britannia Company, a producer of plated flatware. The Wallingford community members simply decided to try what their neighbors were doing with the result that tableware manufacturing was added to the stable of Oneida Community products.

Upon the break-up of the Oneida Community in 1881, all that the former members of the commune possessed were shares of stock in something called Oneida Community, Ltd. The many manufacturing assets of the Community, latterly including table flatware, were carefully preserved, expanded and adapted to changing conditions by a succession of managements led by ex-community members. Along with this industrial activity, the successor company—Oneida Community, Ltd.—also set an example for industrial relations by consistent concern for the welfare of its employees, their income, recreation, retirement and living conditions. None of this was done out of a sense of paternalism. Rather it was a hold-over from the original Oneida Community's belief in the equal honor of all labor and the right of all members to share in the success of the enterprise. The governing rubric was "nobody wealthy—nobody poor." As a part of this philosophy, the city of Sherrill was progressively laid out by the company in quarter-acre lots to accommodate its expanding employment with the company providing the land, utilities, and other infrastructure at a cost which made it possible for employees to own a good home.

In 1915, a union organizer visited Sherrill and reported, in part, as follows:

> I have investigated the Oneida Community Ltd. Silverware factory with the following results: I find this company is perfectly independent of any affiliation with any of the manufacturers' organizations, either in their own line or any other. They work their men short hours, give them good pay and treat them like human beings. Consequently, there is the best of good will between the employer and the employee...The employees seem to be perfectly satisfied with things as they are in the factory. Therefore, I do not believe that any successful organization could be formed among them...
>
> In fact, the company makes a study of its employees in order to give them every opportunity of having good, clean amusements and all kinds of athletics, picture shows, lectures,

bowling, baseball, football, and, in fact, all kinds of outside and inside athletics and amusements that are good for any normal person.

Those are a few of the reasons for the contentment of the employees of this company. I could go on and enumerate a great many more, but I believe enough has been said to convince you that this company is different from any company you have ever heard of in their treatment of their employees. It is not done for advertising purposes, as a great many of our corporations do, but is simply a business policy carried out by men who put the man and woman ahead of the dollar.

There was never a labor union at Oneida Ltd. and no need for such right up to its bankruptcy in 2006. In the course of its pre-bankruptcy existence, Oneida Ltd. had concentrated on the least and last of the original Oneida Community's enterprises—tableware—and eventually succeeded in producing 25% of all silverplated spoons and forks made in the country—a market that had once been a virtual monopoly held by New England manufacturers. Along the way, it divested such original businesses as silk thread production, commercial fruit and vegetable canning, luggage manufacturing, and, in 1925—the manufacture of Newhouse and Victor animal traps—all the products that had made the original community prosperous.

This story has been told by my grandfather, Pierrepont Noyes, the individual most responsible for the direction and success of Oneida Community, Ltd. His 1958 autobiography, *A Goodly Heritage*, describes how he and some other very young men born into the Oneida Community managed to preserve the Community's manufacturing assets and its ideal of selflessness by translating them into a very successful commercial enterprise producing, along the way, the city of Sherrill, N. Y., a lasting monument to their inherent values and careful planning.

I depend on that work for background summarized in the opening chapters, but I also draw on a manuscript written by Pierrepont's half-brother, Holton Noyes, an unpublished corporate history running to over the 237 pages. Holton's "A History of the Oneida Community, Limited" catalogues thoroughly the commercial development of the Oneida Ltd. from its corporate beginnings in 1881 to about 1930 with an exacting choice of words (his portrait of Pierrepont is quoted) which makes me wish he had written more.[1]

A very modest man, Holton Noyes would have resisted putting himself forward in such a way. When, in the 1930s, New York Governor H. Lehman was looking for an administrator of agricultural marketing, Holton was recommended for the job by his brother. Later, Lehman told Pierrepont Noyes that Holton had solved the Governor's biggest problem.

Both Pierrepont Noyes and Holton Noyes devoted considerable effort to describing the top personnel in company management. My own experience at Oneida Ltd. convinced me they were right to do so because company direction and ethos depend to a great extent on the character of those running the show. In this book, therefore, I follow their precedent of paying close attention to Oneida's general managers and presidents.

Both Pierrepont Noyes and Holton Noyes took from their Oneida Community childhoods an uncompromising commitment to honesty in all dealings. Carried over into their adult lives of commerce, that translated into an insistence on integrity and accountability within their business circle. Again, I think they got it right and I fear I imbibed a little of their zealousness for rectitude. At any rate, years after Oneida's final years of frenetic buy-outs and frantic sell-offs always conducted, as it seemed, without full disclosure—even now I feel saddened and outraged. But I am getting ahead of my story.

The late 1950s saw a profound threat to the silverplated business emerge in the form of inexpensive stainless steel flatware made in Japan. In the U.S., the dominant silverplate manufacturer in the U.S. was the International Silver Company controlling over 50% of the market. With its very profitable sterling silver business and an active program of diversification underway, International Silver seemed well placed to meet the challenge of foreign competition. Oneida, in contrast, was totally dependent upon its declining silverplated product. To survive, the company would have to figure out how to make stainless steel flatware profitable at competitive cost.

Oneida did so and, within just a few years, left all traditional flatware rivals in its wake. Not only did Oneida assume unrivaled leadership in the mass marketing of household stainless flatware, it held that position for a period of over forty years. This is a wonderful example of an American company facing a life-threatening challenge, developing a multi-faceted plan, assembling all necessary resources and triumphing in spectacular fashion.

And then, after all these years of survival and success, the company's management responded to an ongoing competitive threat from East Asian manufacturers by extravagant borrowing for dubious acquisitions. A spending binge in the summer of 2000 added $185 million to Oneida's long term debt which had stood at $98 million at the end of January, at which time stockholders equity totaled $133 million.[2] At this point, with total debt exceeding $280 million, far greater than stockholder's equity, the creditors were de facto in control of the business. Soon enough, Oneida Ltd. could not make timely debt payments, waivers were secured, company assets had liens attached, and then those assets were sold in a desperate attempt to raise cash. Employee amenities such as described by the 1915 union organizer were put on the block along with company-owned land in the neighboring community area that had been set aside for eventual development according to long established practices.

With massive debt repayments and insufficient cash generation, the company lost control of the ability to run its own affairs and had not the financial wherewithal or time to adjust once more to foreign competition. An attempt to reduce manufacturing cost was cut short, large lay-offs came into fashion, advertising budgets were reduced, and the Oneida name was freely used on imported product—all to no avail. Between January 31, 2001 and May 31, 2003, debt of $281,896,000 had to be repaid to lenders. This was to be found from a business generating a profit of $20 million at the operating level before interest and taxes in fiscal year 2001.[3]

Had the company practiced its traditional financial conservatism, it may well have been able to survive the Far Eastern threat just as it had survived dire threats in times past. A successful company response probably would have entailed, eventually, a considerable reduction of manufacture. However, a significant cadre of workers and their irreplaceable skills would have been maintained producing high-end products and products for special situations. This circumstance would have provided the means of resurgence should future market conditions change. In any event, a more orderly process of reduced factory production would have avoided bankruptcy, preserved shareholder value, and provided for orderly personnel reconfiguration, rather than the rush out the exits which ensued. It is instructive to remember that in 1962, when the company was faced with declining sales in its major product line of silverplated flatware,

Oneida's financial position made possible a long and costly transition to stainless steel flatware. In that year, Stockholders Equity was nearly $19 million (half in cash) and Total Liabilities were below $1.5 million. Compare this with the situation in FY 2003 when Stockholders Equity was $129 million and Total Liabilities were $396 million![4] What happened at Oneida Ltd. seemed to me a classic case history of failed management abetted by, at best, a complacent board of directors.

Although Oneida Ltd. continued on for several years as an importer and marketer of tableware products, and although it is still housed in the crumbling Tudor administration building built in 1926, it is but a remnant of its former self. Hedge funds now own the company and might sell it once a few good years of operating results are achieved. As a privately held company, there is no way for the public to know how and whether the present corporate incarnation is prospering. (NB: Oneida Ltd. was sold in November 2011 by four hedge funds to an equity fund called EveryWare Global, Inc.)

President Franklin D. Roosevelt once called for an economic bill of rights guaranteeing everyone a job, a living wage, decent housing, medical care, education, and protection from the fears of old age. This the original Oneida Community had done and its ideals were carried over into the commercial enterprise by its descendants who built upon the Community's residual commercial assets. Although Oneida Ltd. provided no formal guarantee, the welfare of its employees was always uppermost in management's mind and manifested in such things as competitive wages, worker bonuses, short time rather than layoffs, paid vacations, pensions, visiting nurses, planned and subsidized housing development, company subsidized schools and public utilities, and employee recreational facilities. And all this was done through the hell-and-high water of nationwide economic ups and downs, rigorous and entrenched competition, two world wars plus Korea and Vietnam. The company not only came through it all but became preeminent in its industry. Then, after over a hundred years of strenuous, successful struggle, Oneida Ltd. came unglued in less than a decade.

I celebrate the remarkable achievements and successful history of pre-bankrupt Oneida in this book. I then follow its sad and unnecessary end because it is a tragedy that should not be forgotten. It should not be shoved down what George Orwell, in the nightmarish vision he described in the novel *1984*, called the Memory Hole.

I was myself a company official, one trained to think about business in economic terms in the trenches of real bottom-line accounting. Since retirement in 1995, I have pored over annual reports and whatever clues to company decision-making may be gleaned from newspaper notices and company announcements. So, while this is a company reminiscence, it is also a financial analysis. It is my interpretation of what happened and why.

While working on this book in 2008, I called the former company president on the phone to ask how—in the opinion of the official who had led Oneida Ltd. into bankruptcy—Oneida's collapse came about. His response was: What's there to talk about?

We might have discussed a recent article in *Fortune* magazine about causes of business failure.

> Why do companies fail? Their CEOs offer every excuse in the book: a bad economy, market turbulence, a weak yen, hundred-year floods, perfect storms, competitive subterfuge—forces, that is, very much outside their control. In a few cases, such as the airlines' post-September 11th problems, the excuses even ring true. But a close study of corporate failure suggests that, acts of God aside, most companies fail for one simple reason: management error.[5]

We also could have discussed how his plan for paying off over $250 million in long-term debt could have been accomplished in three years. Perhaps we could have discussed whether what he was calling "fiduciary responsibility" can be interpreted to mean silence on the subjects of wiping out shareholders and terminating workers? That, at any rate, might have been a good beginning to our conversation.

Notes to Introduction

1   The quotation ("I have investigated") is from Esther Lowenthal, "The Labor Policy of the Oneida Community Ltd.," *Journal of Political Economy* 35 (no. 1, 1927):124-25.

   The story of the Oneida Community and Oneida Community Ltd. is chronicled in Pierrepont B. Noyes, *A Goodly Heritage* (New York: Rinehart,

1958) and in Holton V. Noyes, "A History of the Oneida Community, Limited" (unpublished typescript, Oneida Community Mansion House Archives, ca. 1930). I have also consulted Walter D. Edmonds, *The First Hundred Years, 1848-1948* (Oneida: Oneida Ltd., 1948).

2   Oneida Ltd. Annual Report for Fiscal Year Ending January 29, 2001, 23.
3   Oneida Ltd. Annual Report for Fiscal Years Ending January 29, 2000, 14, and January 24, 2001, 23.
4   Oneida Ltd. Annual Report for Fiscal Years Ending January 21, 1962 and January 25, 2003, 15.
5   Ram Charan and Jerry Useem, "Why Companies Fail," *Fortune*, May 27, 2002; http://www.Fortune.com/indext.Jhtml?channel=print_article.jhtmltdoc_id=207919.

1

Pierrepont B. Noyes, 1897-1950

Age 33, 1930

In the summer of 1948, a huge celebration was staged in Sherrill's Noyes Park to commemorate the one hundred years since the founding of the Oneida Community. During these intervening years the utopian community had been voluntarily abandoned and succeeded by a commercial enterprise called Oneida Community, Ltd. This latter incorporated the productive assets of the original Community and many of its principles and people. A young man now grown old, Pierrepont B. Noyes, born in the Community, had overseen the development of the company from a producer of various products to a major manufacturer of silverplated flatware. At 78 years of age, he was still at the head of the company he had been leading since 1897.

Filling the park, several thousand employees and their families celebrated the occasion in a city that did not exist when Noyes took command of the company. For those with a historical bent, the place where it all began—the Oneida Community's home, the Mansion House—was open to visitors to tour and take in displays about life in the old days. For those who wanted to see how things were produced, tours of the company's factories were available. Speeches were minimal, goodwill was abundant, a good time was had by all ages. In the evening Tommy Dorsey played his theme song, "I'm Getting Sentimental Over You" to dancers under the stars. It was surely a sentimental occasion for many who were there and especially those who had been involved in the evolution of the great enterprise from modest and shaky beginnings to solid and promising circumstance.

Noyes was born in the Mansion House in 1870, a son of the Community's founder, John Humphrey Noyes.[1] Formal education in the Community could be problematic; nonetheless, a love of learning and "improvement" was instilled and not just in its younger generation. Adult education classes were also a regular feature of Community life. A number of Community children would later graduate from various colleges following the Community's break-up in 1881.

As Noyes was well short of the academic background necessary for college admission and with little chance of getting it locally, in 1886 he entered a preparatory school, Colgate Academy, located in Hamilton, N. Y. Based on year-end exams, he was able to skip the next year and return as a senior. In the fall of 1887, he returned to Hamilton but, in a fit of nostalgia for the friends of his youth, he dropped out in November and entered the Loomis Academy which had been started in the home of the former Community where Professor Loomis had been hired to teach the 27 ex-Community children. Noyes wanted to be with them.

Graduating from the Loomis Academy, he was able to enter Madison University (now known as Colgate University), a school dedicated to producing Baptist preachers. After two years at Madison, Noyes had run through the entire non-theological curriculum and, not wishing to enter the ministry, he traveled to Cambridge, Massachusetts, in the summer of 1890 to see about entering Harvard. Despite being rebuffed by a secretary, he managed to reach the dean in charge of admission and worked out an arrangement whereby he would return in September to be tested on various subjects. If he passed, he could then study Harvard's junior year curriculum on his own at home. Following this solitary effort, he would again be tested to see if he had passed his "junior year" and could then become a senior at Harvard.

Noyes returned to Harvard three weeks ahead of the initial qualifying period. After intensive cramming, he was able to pass five Latin exams, four Greek exams, five math exams and one exam each in French, German and Roman/Greek history. Having never studied Greek history previously, he read the text the night before the examination. He had taught himself German in three weeks.

Returning home, Noyes set about tackling the course work for the junior year. Unfortunately, his mother sickened in the spring of 1891 and was diagnosed as terminally ill. Devastated by this news, he abandoned his studies and dedicated himself to caring for his mother. So ended his formal education although he eventually did receive a college degree. After many years of service on its board of trustees and 60 years after entering its Academy, Noyes was awarded the honorary degree of Doctor of Humane Letters from Colgate University.

Following his mother's death and a year of factory work at Oneida, he set off with his brother, Holton, for New York City in 1892. Their plan was simple: make a fortune by playing the stock market. Soon enough, they were stripped of their modest capital and disabused of that ambition. Fortunately, they were helped by a cousin, Mr. George Miller (the New York agent for Oneida Community products), who bolstered their partnership ("Noyes Brothers"), then set them up to sell silverware to restaurants and small stores.

In this sell-or-starve situation, Noyes learned a great deal about persuasion and persistence. He was able to increase his territory to include Upstate New York and some of Pennsylvania and began to generate some large orders. Accordingly, Mr. Miller increased the scope of Noyes' sales activities. Noyes was then able to sell steel traps and chains along with silverware to wholesalers and large department stores located in New England and several large East Coast cities. On top of this, he became a director of the company when his Uncle Abram temporarily gave up *his* seat on Oneida's board in 1894. This gave Pierrepont Noyes, at a young age, an insight into the company's operations that was to be fateful.

Most members of Oneida's board of directors had recently taken up the popular, late 19th-century fad of Spiritualism. Given the board's general lack of business background—with or without visitations from the spirit world—it was no wonder that company profits were suffering. Along with several "non-spiritualist" directors, Noyes conducted a stock fight which he won by a very narrow margin at the stockholders meeting of 1895. Now with a majority of shareholders behind him, Noyes was made manager of the Niagara Falls department which produced table flatware—the eventual future of the company.

Despite managerial responsibilities, he enlarged his sales work to all lines of product and categories of trade—retail, mail order (Sears & Roebuck), restaurants, and premiums—whatever it took to keep the factory busy. However, in the course of running the factory, he learned of troubling conditions which were to re-ignite the attitude and experience of his communitarian youth. Before long, the new knowledge would lead him to create a different kind of company—a company with a concern for the welfare of all its people as well as an equitable distribution of its profits.

Holton Noyes described the character of Pierrepont Noyes in this fashion:

> Physically, his equipment was perfect. His wonderful constitution enabled him to thrive under an enormous load of work. He was never sick and seldom tired.
>
> He had the very happy faculty of throwing aside his cares and entering joyfully into recreations in his hours of relaxation. Temperamentally, he was a glowing optimist, always expecting the best and never discouraged by setbacks. He considered them purely temporary, promptly forgot them and turned his attention to the future. He enjoyed fighting but was never quarrelsome, and he had the rare faculty of fighting relentlessly but never holding a grudge against his adversary. He appreciated the good in his associates and promptly forgot the bad.
>
> He was without any definite religious creed. He belonged to no church, and, so far as I am able to remember, never revealed his beliefs.
>
> Malice and envy had no place in his make-up. Commercially, he was a genius. A wonderful salesman and manager himself, he had that enthusiasm which is contagious. His associates lived upon his vitality. He was a perfect negotiator, never losing sight

of his own purpose and yet fairly recognizing the viewpoint of his adversary.

Above all, he had vision and courage. His ambitions and energies were all for the Oneida Community, Ltd. and only incidentally for himself. He took his pay largely in the satisfaction which follows accomplishment and in the personal joy of seeing his young associates move forward to success. He could use the very firm hand of discipline when necessary, but much preferred the positive hand of encouragement. With all this energy and enthusiasm, his philosophical nature kept his perspective true. He saw things as they actually were and never allowed himself to become inflated with success. In later years, some members of the older generation felt that an all-wise providence had been watching over the affairs of the Oneida Community, Ltd. and had prepared a son of the old Oneida Community with almost ideal qualifications for the new leadership. With his new leadership, religion vanished from O.C.L. business affairs but political and business morality advanced to new and higher standards.[2]

"He has few dislikes," another observer of Noyes added. "Only two that amount to anything. One is wealth and the other is poverty."[3]

Along with his Niagara Falls responsibilities, the 26-year-old Noyes was put in charge of a committee to revitalize the animal trap business at Oneida. Although factory wages were increased overall, manufacturing costs were cut sufficiently to permit price competition as necessary.

At this time, Oneida Community, Ltd. offered a wide range of products: canned fruit and vegetables from its farm, steel traps and chains, refined silk sewing thread and finally, tableware. Profits from Niagara Falls had rescued the company in 1897. Nonetheless, with but three sales agencies and one salesman, Noyes had to spend much of his own time selling. His practice was to stay on the road until he got enough orders to keep his factories running.

In 1897, Noyes became general manager, thus effectively in charge of all company operations. His undeniable success, demonstrable ability, and dedication to Oneida Community values withstood suggestions that he was too young for such responsibility. It is interesting to note that, two years later, a rival chain company was purchased whose cost so alarmed the directors as to produce this sentiment: "We are now prepared to devote our net earnings, above our running expenses, and a reasonable dividend, almost entirely to getting receipts in full from our creditors, until the last dollar of our indebtedness is discharged."[4] That noble ambition would be abandoned one hundred years later.

1899 saw the first and only labor strike in the company's history. Facing down a union organizing attempt at Niagara Falls, Noyes stood by a promise to his workers that he had a plan that would benefit them far beyond what any union could do for them. Events were to prove him right. Following this episode, he was again on the road opening up distribution on the West Coast and in Canada. However, he also oversaw the expansion of employee benefits in such areas as health care, housing, work breaks, and recreation. He would later write about this period that "the Community's conviction that 'life is more than meat' carried over to another generation."[5] And with the strike and all else, the company had its best year ever.

In 1898, a nine-hour day for ten-hours pay had been instituted in Niagara Falls and was extended to Oneida, along with an 11% pay increase. By 1903, wages had increased some 30-40% which, when combined with an expensive advertising campaign to introduce Community Plate, frightened some of the older board members. On top of this, the company had begun a program of employee housing expansion which led, by 1905, to a formal plan for laying out on Community farm land what was to become the City of Sherrill. Housing lots were large, charges to employees were modest, money was loaned by Oneida Community, Ltd. directly or mortgages arranged, and housing bonuses were provided. The result was attractive and affordable housing for people whose labor made the company possible, successful, and profitable.

By 1902, Noyes was working out, along with his youthful management cohorts, his theory for a "semi-socialistic manufacturing institution" and the necessary business plan to keep it alive. He had already given up his early ambition to become wealthy.

Now, he believed "semi-socialism" would provide adequate executive salaries. But with it would be instituted a program for workers that would give them generous hourly wages, profit sharing ahead of dividend increases, and other benefits on the basis of "fair play and because they are deserved." As Noyes summarized: "Act always and only because you believe that Company success should add to the comfort and happiness of every member of the working group."[6] This principle was to guide the company for most of its existence.

In 1900, after surveying the company's diverse range of products, it was decided that only silverplated flatware offered the prospect of sufficient growth in volume and profit to fulfill the ambition the young management team had for the company. Unfortunately, silverware was dominated by established New England manufacturers with well known trademarks. To break into that market, an extensive advertising campaign to promote "Community Plate" was undertaken and product quality was improved. Profits from trap and chain sales were to pay for it all until silverware became profitable in its own right.

The earliest years of the century were a time of building and experimentation. First, distinctive patterns were introduced. Second, the quality of Community Plate was upgraded to "triple plus," far above the level of competitive offerings. Pricing policy assuring dealer profit was introduced and the sales staff was expanded. Sales of other products were pushed to ensure sufficient total company profit to fund a Community Plate advertising budget of $30,000—*six times* what the board had been anticipating! Thus, 1903 ended what Noyes described as "three years of study and experiment before we took the final plunge."[7]

And then, in 1904, Berton L. "Doc" Dunn appeared on the scene. A child of the Oneida Community like Noyes, he had become an ear, nose, and throat physician with a practice in Syracuse. He gave it up to join the company and turned out to be an advertising genius whose insight and taste put Community Silver on the map. In fact, Doc's innovations and advertising theories were later widely imitated: use of valuable props (e.g., museum lace), full-page color ads, employment of famous artists, reduced copy, endorsement by well known authorities (e.g., Mrs. Vanderbilt), superb photography, and campaign continuity. All of this promoted the purchase of an excellent but unknown product at both trade and consumer levels across the land.

Noyes saw the need for organizational development and the need, as well, for talented "joiners." This was very much in the tradition of the old Community and allowed the company to attract superior people from every possible source. The future course of the company was effectively set as early as 1901. A young but seasoned management team, enriched by a bevy of "joiners," was in place to both secure the established manufacturing and marketing base and to push expansion in flatware.

Further advancement was threatened by a financial downturn in 1907 which caused a decline in profit of over 60% in 1908. The company, however, did not "panic" during the abrupt recession. On the contrary, advertising expenditures were maintained at a high level with the result that the company picked up sales from faint-hearted competitors. Profits quickly recovered and reached new heights in 1909. Profits rose again, by 30%, in 1910. That year, P. B. Noyes was unanimously elected company president at the age of 39 years.

During the period 1910-17, Oneida Community, Ltd. continued to grow in sales and profits. Along with this—and possibly because of it—the company increased both dividends and social expenditures for such things as school buildings and recreational facilities. Furthermore, it was decided in 1913 to relocate both the tableware factory from Niagara Falls, N. Y., to Sherrill along with any workers who wanted to stay with Oneida. Within a year, a new factory building was constructed along with housing for the transferred employees. The board of directors had been enlarged by five younger executives in 1911 and, a year later, the chain making business was sold, its future prospects not looking bright. Canadian manufacture of silverware was inaugurated in 1916 and, in the same year, the silk business was sold. Competition had eaten into its profits of silk and its sale proceeds were welcome help for expanding the silverware department.

Sales declined from another economic downturn coinciding with the beginning of World War I in 1914. As a result, executive salaries were cut in half, other wages were reduced, and the factory was put on short time. In 1916, employees were repaid what they had lost in wages and short time. When the company entered the war, it also gave its employees a separate weekly pay packet to compensate them for the prevailing inflation. This extra bonus eventually came to about 50% of employees' base pay.

Working on his theory of turning management over to the next generation as soon as possible, Noyes had appointed Albert "Ab" Kinsley as General Manager in 1917. At that point, Noyes—still President at age 46—went to California for an extended stay while Ab settled in. The California sojourn was interrupted by the U. S. entry into the war, and Noyes returned to Oneida to oversee the company's response to the crisis. To ensure that company employees entering armed services would not suffer financially, the company worked out a plan to make up the difference between military pay and what the employee's average income had been in the factory.

Noyes shared with many the conviction that this war pitted democracy against totalitarianism. Therefore, as soon as he was satisfied that company management had things well in hand, he patriotically went to Washington looking to do volunteer work for the national effort. Noyes became a member of the Fuel Administration in which he made the acquaintance of Bernard Baruch. When the conflict ended in 1918, Noyes traveled to Italy on business, but he stopped over in Paris where he encountered the World War I peace conference in session. There he ran into Baruch who, it turned out, was looking for an American to serve on the Rhineland Commission, a four-country directorate charged with overseeing the occupation of former German territory. Baruch thought Noyes would be perfect for the job.

Pierrepont Noyes and his son, Pete Noyes, 1937

The result was that Noyes and his family spent over a year in Coblenz, Germany. In later years, he would remember with pride that his direct appeal to President Wilson for a civilian-controlled occupation of the Rhineland provinces was approved despite the French demand for a punitive military occupation. Coblenz proved to be a fascinating interlude for an amateur diplomat cast among famous and infighting professionals.

Although mostly absent from Oneida during 1917-20, Noyes was still President and he continued to follow events there. The post-war business boom alarmed him and he urged, in 1920, a course of corporate caution and liquidity. However, he had to admit that, in view of excellent sales, he was being, perhaps, overly cautious. When—as he feared—the boom ended abruptly in 1921, incoming orders greatly diminished as orders in-house were cancelled in great numbers. By January 1922, the company had lost $500,000 and had had to secure loans from the bank totaling $2,000,000.

1925 saw Ab Kinsley resign, later to return to the company. During his general managership, Kinsley put in place many innovations that enhanced the welfare of employees: a lucrative wage bonus scheme, contributions to the Sherrill school system, housing bonuses, substantial investment to bring abundant and good water to the area, and extensive recreational facilities under the control of Community Associated Clubs—all accomplished in five years.

Business recovered and again boomed until 1929. Following Kinsley's resignation, Noyes had agreed to directly manage the company until a General Manager was elected. The person elected was his son-in-law, an outstanding executive whose story is the subject of the next chapter.

With his reduced executive duties, Noyes occupied his time in various ways. In 1921 he had written his first book, *While Europe Waits for Peace*, an autobiography of his Rhineland experiences which foresaw another European war in about 25 years. In the early 1920s, he had given many talks urging that the country join the League of Nations.

Waking from a dream in 1927, he wrote a science fiction novel (*The Pallid Giant*) which presciently describes the destruction of an ancient civilization by atomic weapons due to "fears of other men's fears". He would, in 1936, write his well received autobiography, *My Father's House*, about his youthful upbringing in the Oneida Community—a book that found an audience at home and abroad. His literary undertakings concluded with his 1958 work about company history (*A Goodly Heritage*). Along the way, he found time to serve as a trustee of Colgate University which conferred to him in 1946 the honorary degree of Doctor of Humane Letters.

In 1930, his old friend Bernard Baruch advised New York's then Governor, Franklin Roosevelt, to put Noyes in charge of a large development at the Saratoga Spa. Noyes was told that his attention to this project would only take a few days or—at most—a year. In the event, it led to monthly visits to Saratoga for the next 22 years during the construction and administration of this magnificent enterprise that included the Roosevelt Baths and Campus.

When Noyes resigned on August 1, 1950, he could look back on 40 years as company president with satisfaction. His dreams and those of his young associates had been fulfilled. After becoming effective head of the company in 1897, he had seen the firm develop from a manufacturer of animal traps, sewing silk, canner of fruits and vegetables and maker of cheap flatware, into the second leading producer of tableware in the country. Along the way and just as importantly, the local community had evolved as he had hoped. The city of Sherrill had been planned and employees assisted to live there. Utilities, schools and extensive recreational facilities had been established for the citizenry. Good wages and good benefits were paid to employees and good enough salaries to executives. Noyes' idea of nobody being rich and nobody being poor was in place and the company's future looked bright.

When Noyes stepped down, Miles E. "Dunc" Robertson became president and also retained the position he had held since 1926 as General Manager. Some measure of how far the company had progressed was afforded by an announcement, the same day, that William A. Rogers, a relatively small division of Oneida Ltd., would be holding sales meetings the following week which involved three sales managers and 26 salesmen! (In those days, the company's salesmen were called "agents." Later, the company would come to rely on independent agents instead of its own sales force.)

Noyes died April 15, 1959. His service in the Big Hall of his beloved Mansion House was held in the tradition of the Oneida Community. The "meeting" was led by a local minister and anyone who felt called upon said what they thought or remembered of this remarkable human being. An obituary had this to say: "With the passing last week of Pierrepont B. Noyes, 89, Madison County's most prominent industrialist, most distinguished public servant and one of her best loved individuals, an era came to an end."[8]

Notes to Chapter 1

1. Noyes' life is summarized from Pierrepont B. Noyes' *A Goodly Heritage* (New York: Rinehart, 1958).
2. Holton V. Noyes, "A History of the Oneida Community, Limited," unpublished typescript (Oneida Community Mansion House Archives, ca. 1930), 114-15.
3. G. R. N., "The Community Album," *Community Quadrangle* 2, no. 2 (April 1927), 13.
4. H. V. Noyes, "A History of the Oneida Community, Limited," 151 (quote at March 1899).
5. P. B. Noyes, *Goodly Heritage*, 161.
6. P. B. Noyes, *Goodly Heritage*, 173, 175-76.
7. P. B. Noyes, *Goodly Heritage*, 192.
8. *Oneida Daily Dispatch*, about April 20, 1959.

2 | Miles E. Robertson, 1926-1959

Miles "Dunc" Robertson

Miles E. "Dunc" Robertson was born in Canastota in 1889 to a farm family residing just west of Peterboro, N. Y. His early schooling began in a one-room school house. However, as his parents wanted their children to receive a high school education, a residence was built north of the canal in Canastota to which the family relocated. Since the new home was nine miles from the family farm, the logistics of attending to the family business were formidable. This got Robertson into running at an early age cross-country from the farm in Canastota.

His progress through high school was interrupted by a dispute with the principal. When his father ordered him to apologize to that official, Robertson refused. His father then told him that he could not "put his feet under the dining table" until he decided otherwise. Robertson responded by leaving home for a time to work building the West Shore Railroad's "Third Rail." A year of doing that helped to change his mind and he returned to both school and the family table.

Upon graduation, he entered Syracuse University to study law thinking he could then partner with his older brother who had set up a law office in Canastota. He did not join a fraternity his first year, as he assumed that a poor farm boy in an ill-fitting suit would not be wanted. Living in a boarding house where the food served was on the basis of "you pays for what you gets, not what you wants," he supplemented his diet by playing three intercollegiate sports. That meant always being on the training table where the food was good, plentiful and, above all, free.

Once he had established himself, he joined Beta Theta Pi fraternity, presumably a cut above those that might have chosen him in his feral state. Always competitive, Robertson supplemented his modest funds by shooting pool. Later, he continued to do this as a young salesman for Oneida Community, Ltd.

During summer vacations, Robertson also competed in field days where cash awards were made to the winners of various races. An old and yellowed news clipping relates how he "was the winner in every event that he entered" in a field day at Clarks Mills, and also carried home several "prizes," presumably with some cash. "Canastota has every reason to feel proud of Miles Edgar Robertson," a newspaper reported at the time, "who has just been named as the 'ideal Syracuse University junior student.' This honor is about the best Syracuse University affords. Qualifications cover scholarship, athletics and other collegiate activities."[1]

As soon as he graduated from Syracuse's law school in 1912, Robertson passed the bar examination. He then spent a year working at his brother's law business. He discovered, soon enough, that he did not like law as a full-time profession. As he cast about looking for a new start, he happened to land a job for six months in the legal department of Oneida Community, Ltd.

From this start, he became a field salesman for Oneida and, after a couple of years, a district sales manager. Next, from 1917-19, Robertson went into export sales. With time out for a brief military career in World War I, he became sales manager for that department and traveled the world during the period 1920-21. Switching back to domestic sales, he was assistant sales manager from 1922-24, becoming a board member in 1923. His appointment as Assistant General Manager in 1924 led to his promotion to General Manager in 1926.

Robertson, at this point, had had ten years of selling and sales management, three years of general management training, and the opportunity to view and discuss corporate matters that came before the Board of Directors. When General Manager Ab Kinsley resigned in 1925, Noyes had said that he would assume his duties for one year only.

A fully qualified Robertson was ready to take over corporate operational leadership as general manager when that year was over. Pierrepont Noyes was only too willing to turn the day-to-day operations of the company over to this highly intelligent, competitive, and well-trained executive who also happened to be his son-in-law—Robertson had married Pierrepont's daughter, Constance, in 1918.

Oneida Community, Ltd. in 1926 seemed solidly profitable having just constructed a new and remarkably handsome Canadian factory overlooking Niagara Falls. Also, the company was about to purchase, for $300,000, the William A. Rogers tableware company located on the American side of the falls. This, among other things, would bring to the buyer several useful Rogers trademarks along with the Heirloom silver brand. The company further expanded by purchasing the Simeon L. and George H. Rogers Company located in Connecticut. The latter firm also had a factory in Northampton, Massachusetts, that produced knives (closed in 1939). All acquired manufacturing activity was, except for Northampton, transferred to Oneida. The result of this activity was that the company entered the fateful year of 1929 with corporate debt totaling $500,000.

Following the stock market crash and ensuing Depression, both the country and the company hit rock bottom economically in 1932. By that point, the corporate dividend had been eliminated, the factory put on short time, executive salaries cut in half, jobs "restructured," and austerity practiced in every area. Robertson's draconian measures were so severe that he feared he and his wife would have to leave town due to the resentment caused by his cutback measures. Not so—people were grateful to have work even if it was only part time. Owing in large measure to Robertson's leadership, the company actually made a profit in 1933 unlike any other tableware manufacturer and most other companies.

Continuing to make money, the company restored the dividend in 1935. However, the severe economic downturn in 1937 returned the country to previous poor economic conditions. "Production and trade averaged about the same as 1935" or "it fell to a point about midway between the 1929 peak and 1932 low" was how Oneida's 1939 annual report characterized conditions. In the same report, the company's treasurer, Louis Wayland-Smith, could state "our financial condition is excellent with current assets twelve times the current liabilities, and cash above twice current liabilities from the bottom of the depression six years ago.... The company has increased net worth by $1,102,000...making dividend payments of $1,688,000. Bonded debt of $1,284,500 and bank loans of $400,000 have been entirely paid up." Also, cash on hand increased by $300,000.[2] All this occurred during a year in which the nation's commerce went severely downhill. Keep this in mind for future reference.

Sales picked up in succeeding years until 1942 when World War II started in earnest. Although preferred and common dividends were being paid at the usual rate, an extra dividend (a recent innovation) was omitted as the company worked to strengthen its cash position given the uncertainties of a full year at war. The extra dividend had perhaps been compensation for dividends omitted when times had been tough. Employee bonuses had started again in 1937 and were continued along with customary contributions to employee welfare programs. However, the cash position was reduced by inventories of war-related materials for recently acquired government contracts while access to raw materials for tableware production became difficult.

The company looked forward to getting its share of future war-related work. Logically enough, the company was then producing surgical instruments for the government. Optimistically, Oneida continued its normal consumer advertising expenditures for tableware and planned to start making sterling silver.

With the war in full swing, the 1943 annual report announced, "We are no longer silverware manufacturers and our factories are running twenty-four hours a day producing vitally necessary items for the Armed Forces." The company had made an exceedingly quick conversion to wartime production and would go on to produce a variety of war materials which, beyond surgical instruments, included gun parts (bayonets, sights, slide mechanism for the carbine), airplane parts (fuel tanks, elevator controls, shackles for bombs), casings for the M74 Chemical (fire) Bomb, and a bearing essential to the engines of Allied bombers and fighters as well as to American tanks.

By 1945, 700 Oneida employees were in uniform. At the beginning of the conflict, Robertson had these eloquent words to say about how the company and its people should face up to the wartime situation.

War changes our lives in many ways. It makes it difficult at times to know what we should do, how we should act, what we should say. It makes us think in terms of our obligations rather than our privileges, our responsibilities rather than our rights. One thing is certain. Whereas at all times we should work and live together as a team, with good will and mutual understanding, in war time this obligation is even greater. When we have over 450 of our men fighting abroad to protect our way of life, we must make doubly sure to strengthen and preserve it at home.[3]

Throughout the war years, the company expanded and improved its manufacturing plant to meet military production requirements. At the same time, Oneida continued to add to its powerful balance sheet with systematic yearly increases in net worth through 1944, the last full year of war. The company's war contracts were annually audited by the government to root out any excess profits. None were found. Wartime profits, achieved by hard work and good management, were limited by wartime tax regulations.

Committees, in the meantime, had been set up to study the problems of re-conversion to peacetime production. Cash was set aside in reserves for what would be an expensive re-conversion to tableware manufacturing once the war ended.

Company profits indeed declined as anticipated post-war costs of re-conversion kicked in. However, plans were also laid for further factory expansion in 1946 and 1947. The 1946 annual report confidently stated that sales prospects for tableware "are not only good but were never better."[4] Pent-up demand was lying in wait for peacetime production. Financial reserves were at an all-time high.

Still president in 1950, Pierrepont Noyes wrote his last stockholder letter for the annual report. He was happy to report steadily increasing profits based on heavy sales volume, a good mix of high quality goods, and new pattern introductions. What especially pleased him was improved manufacturing methods which lowered costs, improved quality, and eliminated "tough disagreeable operations upon which no worker likes to be employed." In this final letter, Noyes stressed that Oneida was "an unusually personal company" in which profits and safety resulted from "the personal interest of and loyalty of 4,400 workers, salesmen and executives." "Your company," he concluded, "has a wonderful organization."[5]

Further, the company was in good hands and Noyes was tremendously proud of his successor's competence. Robertson, in Noyes' view, was a courageous director whose natural aggressiveness was "always balanced by an instinct which insists upon a careful study of pertinent facts and possibilities of each situation." Noyes gave Robertson credit for having brought the company through the Depression and into profitability sooner than any competitor. Robertson's management had garnered for the company the coveted Army-Navy "E" award for wartime excellence and his supervision of post-war changeover had been superb.

Figures will, perhaps, best tell of the quality of [Robertson's] management. By 1950, Oneida Ltd.'s annual sales were nearly three times the sales made in any year before 1927. Starting in 1933 with no "operating surplus," he had by 1950 built up a surplus of nearly $11,000,000 in addition to wage bonuses, during the period, of nearly $9,000,000. He had made additions to the Pension Fund of $4,400,000 and appropriation of many millions for the furthering of factory, home and recreational improvements, as well as uninterrupted payments of liberal dividends to the stockholders.[6]

And, having imbibed Noyes' ethic of "Nobody rich, nobody poor," Dunc Robertson kept his own pay low. A director who joined the board in

1957, vividly recalled a meeting at which Robertson, company president, adamantly insisted that $25,000 a year was all the salary he wanted. Anything extra, he thought fit to add, should be spread among other executives.[7]

After 24 years as general manager in which he was essentially the administrative head of the company, Robertson became president in 1950. Business conditions were upset that summer with the advent of the Korean War bringing with it imposition of wartime controls and fear for raw material supply. First the trade stocked up, then slowed its purchasing in order to lower inflated retail inventories when consumer sales did not develop as expected. High gross profit lines such as silverplate and sterling silver (introduced after World War II) experienced sales declines. However, reporting on 1953 results, Robertson mentioned stainless steel flatware for the first time. "The greatest growth, both in sales and factory efficiencies, occurred in our stainless steel flatware division. Stainless steel flatware, while at present a short profit line, is of great aid in our efforts to provide full employment."[8] Little did he or anyone else at the time foresee the ultimate profit potential in this "short profit" product and how it would affect the company and its industry.

Dunc Robertson addresses the crowd at the 1948 Centennial event

JOHN P. L. HATCHER

Back in 1943, Oneida rented a factory in Canastota that had once made commercial vehicles. It had been fitted out to make photographic trailers for the Air Force during the war. Purchased in 1945 and re-named Oneida Products Corporation, it became a manufacturer mainly of school buses. The company finally gave up on the Canastota operation and its vicissitudes, selling it at a loss of $300,000 in 1952.

The Company's Financial Position

Every man and woman who works for a company should know what that company's financial position is. Those who work for Oneida Ltd. work here for more than just a "job." On the payroll are many grandfathers, fathers and sons — and families such as these, building a future such as they have in Oneida Ltd., realize as good business people that the company they work with must have a stable and sound financial background. Upwards of 900 Oneida Ltd. employees are stockholders.

WE OWNED (Assets)

CASH—In banks and on hand, with which to pay for materials and supplies, wages, taxes, etc.	$ 1,491,494.21
UNITED STATES AND CANADIAN GOVERNMENT SECURITIES At cost	77,045.00
RECEIVABLES—Money due us, mostly for goods sold, less ample reserves	865,773.11
INVENTORIES—War production contracts in process, stocks of silverware, raw materials and supplies	3,578,313.33
INVESTMENTS—Net worth of our English Subsidiary at the present rate of exchange, less a reserve of $50,000 for contingencies, and stocks of other companies, mortgages, notes, etc., less ample reserves	145,284.88
FUNDS HELD FOR EMPLOYEES FOR PURCHASE OF WAR BONDS	57,023.61
RECEIVABLE FROM UNITED STATES GOVERNMENT—Post-war refund of excess profits tax	11,000.00
PROPERTY, PLANT, AND EQUIPMENT—Land, factory buildings, machinery and equipment, administration and home buildings, houses rented to employees, farms, etc.; after proper allowance for accumulated wear and tear	3,055,212.23
PREPAID EXPENSES—Unexpired insurance premiums, rent paid in advance, advances to salesmen for future traveling expenses, etc.	79,681.12
TOTAL OF WHAT WE OWNED (Assets)	$ 9,360,827.49

...and where the money is....

The Oneida organization has lived through the Civil War, Spanish American War and World War I — and through twelve major country-wide depressions.

Today its financial position is stronger than at any other time in the history of the company.

A detailed statement, as of January 31, 1943, is shown on these pages.

WE OWED (Liabilities)

ACCOUNTS PAYABLE—For raw materials, supplies and services	$ 200,343.03
ACCRUED PAYROLLS AND EXPENSES—Mostly for year-end payrolls to be paid after January 31	111,492.90
EMPLOYEES' WAGE BONUS—A share of the year's profits to be distributed among all employees of over six months' service. (An additional $2,500 has already been paid)	222,500.00
ACCRUED TAXES—Due to Federal, State, and Canadian governments, but not yet paid (after deducting $300,750 representing U. S. Treasury Tax Notes now held, to be applied in payment of taxes)	391,250.00
FUNDS DEPOSITED WITH US BY EMPLOYEES FOR PURCHASE OF WAR BONDS	57,023.61
TOTAL OF WHAT WE OWED (Liabilities)	$ 982,609.54
WHAT WE OWNED LESS WHAT WE OWED (Stockholders' Investment)	$ 8,378,217.95

STOCKHOLDERS' INVESTMENT

PREFERRED STOCKHOLDERS' INVESTMENT At par value	$ 2,400,000.00
COMMON STOCKHOLDERS' INVESTMENT At par value	2,474,000.00
CAPITAL SURPLUS Money now invested in the business resulting from capital stock adjustments	1,028,607.21
EARNED SURPLUS—That part of the earnings of past years which have been left in the business, thus providing necessary working funds	2,075,610.74
RESERVE FOR CONTINGENCIES—Portion of earnings reserved for post-war restoration of facilities and for other contingencies which may arise	400,000.00
TOTAL STOCKHOLDERS' FUNDS AND RESERVES	$ 8,378,217.95

However, Oneida continued through the early 1950s to invest substantially in improved manufacturing methods and equipment and, as always, in national advertising. With the Korean War and a persistent decline of silverplate sales, the company established a Special Products Division in 1954 with the intent of attracting government defense work, something it had been very familiar with a few short years before. The effort would lead to building a factory to produce jet engine blades.

Sales in 1955 followed a bifurcated pattern, good the first half year, poor the second half. Significantly, stainless steel flatware continued its strong growth pattern in the U. S. and Canada. The year as a whole showed profit improvement over the previous years despite the sales force being largely re-arranged into new territories and then having to face stiff competition from "discounters" in the autumn. Continued growth of close-margin stainless steel flatware sales would be cited as the reason for greatly reduced profits in 1956 along with "large development expenses in our growing defense business."

By 1958, Oneida was entirely out of the defense business. The building constructed for that purpose was reconfigured to produce Oneida's first foray into diversification: plastic dishes made of melamine material. Robertson was never enthusiastic about the profit possibilities of this product. Later events were to prove him correct.

Among the complaints aired in the annual report of 1958 was that of strong discount-price competition. Sales in the high-profit line of silverplate were at their worst level since the end of World War II. Although "sales of stainless steel flatware continued strong and healthy," the future of this product would not be easy. "The flood of low-priced foreign imports of stainless steel continued to plague us," and continued to suppress stainless price increases that might have offset declining silverplate sales.

The company began a process of appealing to the tariff commission which led, in 1957, to a voluntary export quota by Japanese manufacturers. (N.B. The company, incidentally. suspected Japan promptly exceeded that limit.) Robertson would continue his representations to the tariff commission with effective results. The first quota remained in effect for several years and, while not renewed immediately after, it was reinstituted in the 1960s. This brought needed relief which permitted Oneida to improve its manufacturing efficiencies, product development, and promotional activity.

Robertson's final year as president was 1959. In March 1960, Pierrepont ("Pete") T. Noyes became president with Robertson remaining on the Board of Directors as its chairman until 1967. In his last annual letter to shareholders, Robertson indicated a significant improvement in net profits. But though sales were up, he warned, gross profits were down due to competitive conditions.[9] Unanticipated Melamine dinnerware start-up costs were to blame for substantial losses. Also reported was the decision to depart Sheffield, England (where plated flatware for the English and Commonwealth markets had been manufactured since the 1920s) and build an integrated factory in Northern Ireland.

As a manager, Robertson favored a hands-on but participative process. Reserving his own opinion, he would gather around him those involved in or liable to be affected by a decision. He would then ask pointed questions about the topic at hand. In the end, he would write up or dictate in front of the group what had been discussed and decided, seeking their concurrence as he went along.

Depending on the project, a series of such meetings might be held to review the project and its development. Always he stressed the availability of guidance and the desirability of follow-up. All relevant personnel had a chance to contribute to the process and "buy in" to the decisions and undertakings. Firm understandings, agreement and assignments emerged from this give-and-take. In its essentials, this procedure resembled the way the original Oneida Community arrived at agreement. It also happens to be the method promoted in the present by many management consultants.

In the ten years of Robertson's presidency, earned surplus increased by more than $3,000,000 to $12,376,343 or 32% despite such financially draining developments during the decade as the secular decline of highly profitable silverplate sales, major investments in plant and equipment, and checkered over-all business conditions.[10] The big development which would be the wave of the company's future emerged during the 1950s: stainless steel flatware. Its growth and eventual preeminence were made possible by the financial reserves which Robertson had carefully put in place over so many years. These reserves would be called upon for heavy investment in manufacturing innovation and equipment along with dominant marketing expenditure.

Robertson remained on Oneida's board until his approaching demise brought about his resignation in August 1972. Just prior to his death, the Board of Directors presented him with a plaque reading:

> Be it resolved that the Board of Directors of Oneida Ltd. express its deep appreciation to Miles E. Robertson for his personal qualities and ideals which were a constant inspiration to his associates.
>
> For his sure and guiding leadership in the affairs of this company especially through the dark days of the depression and war years.
>
> For his vast experience and boundless energy that has contributed so greatly to the success not only of Oneida, but the tableware industry as a whole.
>
> With deep appreciation to our Past President, Chairman, fellow Director and friend.[11]

The local press paid him fulsome tribute. The *Oneida Dispatch*, for example, wrote of his 59 years of total service and 33 years as operational head of Oneida Ltd.—"a front runner in the industry and predominant in the stainless steel tableware field." Robertson, the article made clear, was not only widely admired, he was sincerely liked:

> A lot of qualities in addition to keen intelligence, energy and ability help account for Robertson's outstanding success…He communicates, he commands both popularity and respect… because he likes people and has helped others all his life…What these reflections add up to is simply that Robertson has been such a force for good in our community and far beyond and has had such an impact upon so many lives.[12]

The note Pete Noyes wrote to company employees on the occasion of Robertson's death echoed those sentiments.

> Probably there is no one who was better known longer, nor whoever did more for Oneida Ltd. than Dunc Robertson. Of course, what he did and said was important, but the great thing about him was how he did it. Dunc seemed to know better than most people how to put his thoughts and beliefs into action. As a result, he was not only respected as a leader, but beloved as a friend and advisor.[13]

As Pete once said, "I got my MBA working for Dunc."

Notes to Chapter 2

1. The "old and yellowed news clipping"—unattributed and undated—is in the author's possession. Another clipping lacking attribution, "Honors for Robertson," is internally dated May 9, 1911.
2. Oneida Ltd. Statement, January 31, 1939.
3. Oneida Ltd. Statement, January 31, 1943.
4. Oneida Ltd. Statement, January 31, 1946.
5. Oneida Ltd. Annual Report for Fiscal Year Ended January 31, 1950.
6. Pierrepont B. Noyes, *A Goodly Heritage* (New York: Rinehart, 1958), 264-65.
7. Stuart Hill, personal communication.
8. Oneida Ltd. Annual Report for Fiscal Year Ended January 31, 1954.
9. Oneida Ltd. Annual Report for Fiscal Year Ended January 31, 1959.
10. Information in this section drawn from Oneida Ltd. Annual Reports for Fiscal Years Ended January 31, 1955 through 1960." Large development expenses" quoted from 1957; "our sales of stainless steel" and "the flood of low-priced foreign imports" are from the 1959 report.
11. The plaque presented to Robertson dated August 30, 1972, is in the author's possession.
12. "Thanks, Dunc!," *Oneida Daily Dispatch*, September 7, 1972.
13. "Dear Fellow Employees," letter from Pete Noyes dated October 6, 1972.

3

Stainless Steel

This chapter is about a corporate switch from plated to stainless flatware, an astonishing development spanning the presidencies of Dunc Robertson and his successor, Pete Noyes (subject of the next chapter). Oneida Ltd. had about 25% of the plated silverware market—at its most successful. After War II, however, consumers came to prefer stainless steel cutlery, mostly made abroad at a cost Oneida could not match. These trends not only threatened Oneida's standing as a leading silverware manufacturer, they jeopardized its very survival. Oneida Ltd. responded with innovative technology and designs, and new methods for advertising and marketing the new product. The company emerged from this crisis as the largest maker of stainless flatware in the world.

The success was underwritten by the cash reserves built up by Robertson and fostered by his Socratic method of supervision. It was further encouraged by Noyes. But it happened, apparently, without a master plan and without orders filtering down from above. Oneida's stainless industry evolved gradually from the ground up as different departments worked closely together. It came about because competent and confident mid-level management created it. In what follows, I present the story of Oneida stainless as related to me by those who achieved the success.

At the start of the 1950s, Oneida manufactured a very modest quantity of stainless ware comprising only two lines (Oneida Stainless and Oneidacraft Deluxe) with four patterns. Fifty-piece sets sold for $19.95 to $39.95. The traditional retail distributors—jewelers and silver dealers—were unenthusiastic about the product and its cost.

That led to Oneida focusing on different venues: housewares departments and distributors. In this sector, Oneida found a broad range of products but with emphasis on the major brand in each product category, a high rate of traffic, and the space and willingness to promote. As against silver departments, housewares operated on thinner margins and higher stock turn. This latter required good distributor service to keep the retail store displays filled.

Since wholesale jewelers were attuned to slower-turning products, it was necessary not only to attract housewares distributors to handle Oneida products, but also to train them to do so. This was not easily done because Oneida had no sales history with these distributors. Les Smith, Director of Domestic Sales, often had to sell both product *and* the wholesaler to retail accounts. (Later on, we would also train jewelry distributors.)

In addition to working out new modes of distribution, Oneida developed innovative patterns that made stainless attractive and desirable. Bob Landon, manager of stainless sales and hotel/restaurant, insisted that engineering and the factory could work together to develop a Victorian pattern stainless. Landon's initiative, encouraged by Dunc Robertson, resulted in a 1956 design called *Chateau*—a technological breakthrough in stainless and an immediate success for the ODL (Oneidacraft Deluxe) line. In 1957, *Paul Revere* was introduced in Oneidacraft Premier (a Community Stainless quality). Both of these patterns continued to sell well for a half century.

Under Frank Perry, Oneida began a program of vigorous design introduction and moved away from the early notion that stainless design had to be plain, stark, and "Nordic" looking. In 1964, *Michelangelo* represented an impressive design and quality statement given its intricacy and the thickness of metal upon which it was made. Oneida Ltd. was first with Florentine finish in the 1960s, opening up a range of pattern possibilities. Although second with Mediterranean design (Gorham was first), in the late 1960s, Oneida soon came to dominate this design category.

Everyone worked to achieve high standards, what company people called "OCQ" (Oneida Community Quality). A particularly close partnership between design and engineering gave Oneida the ability to produce intricate patterns on heavier weight stock and in bigger piece sizes than its competition. Engineering went on to develop machines and methods to make the resulting production at competitive cost.

The engineering department was headed by Stewart Hill, "a rare bird," a contemporary called him, "an exceptional engineer who also understood financial management." Hill and his staff literally invented the machinery necessary to efficiently process high quality stainless flatware at competitive cost. When they finished modifying a Clare machine, for example, it did not resemble anything the manufacturer had supplied. Lucien Sprague and Art Pohl were credited for their sensitivity to cost control as was Ivan Becker for his work in making the tools necessary to provide the dimensional control needed to produce intricate design. The innovative use of coining presses (instead of drop hammers) cut wage cost, scrap costs, die and tool costs, and increased output. Other engineering/production breakthroughs that occurred as Oneida Ltd. gained momentum in stainless flatware during the 1950s and 1960s were coil blanking, five-stand rolling and outline cutting, Dial tining, automatic belt tiners, and five- and seven-machine finishing units.

At the same time, new lessons had to be learned about the nature of stainless steel. Beginning with what was called 430 chrome steel, Oneida technicians moved on to 18/8 nickel stainless which gives better finish and rust resistance. However, it took a while to get the best results from this new and hard-to-work metal. Oneida's metal suppliers helped to solve manufacturing problems as they arose. In the end, Oneida had a product line that was superior in finish to anything the competition could offer. Finally, at the end of the process, Andy Beshgetoor and Andy Jubanyik developed an effective method of market-testing new patterns which saved a number of costly and otherwise time-consuming product mistakes.

While Oneida was fortunate to have the engineering strength and leadership to permit maximum exploitation of the available marketing possibilities, it was equally blessed with innovative thinking about advertising. Beginning with the slogan, "Nature makes it carefree, Oneida makes it beautiful," stainless advertising moved on to the eminently successful teaspoon sampling program. Initially, this latter campaign delivered a teaspoon direct to the consumer for 25 cents in whatever pattern was requested. More than 10 million spoons were eventually placed in homes across the country. Consumers could then see for themselves the beauty of this product which, indeed, lived up to a later slogan and suggestion: "Look Again, It's Stainless!" And, the sample spoon served as a constant reminder of Oneida and the desirability of buying a full set of Oneida stainless.

Early on, Oneida Ltd. provided countertop units to dealers in order that they could make an efficient and effective presentation of our products. The biggest and most dramatic was the "Oneida Tabletop Shop" worked up in the spring of 1962 by Jim Colway (Advertising and Sales Promotion) and Vice President Dud Sanderson. This was an innovative, expensive, large, permanent display fixture which would show all of Oneida's patterns and dominate any store department in which it might be placed. Les Smith had it tested in the department store chain of Woodward and Lothrup where it succeeded in generating interest and sales. Over the years, the size and nature of such permanent display units have been modified. However, Oneida never went back on the idea of having a permanent fixture of its own design and identification in retail markets.

The rise of stainless steel was coincident with great improvements in photographic representation of the product and advances in printing processes. Jim Colway saw to it that Oneida always had the best-looking merchandising materials and set packaging in the industry which greatly reinforced the image of the product among both the trade and consumers. Later on, Oneida took on the Deutsch agency and, with it, a full-color advertising format that long kept the Oneida name regularly in front of prospective purchasers in clever and memorable ways. No one, it was widely believed, came close to Oneida Ltd. in terms of the money and messaging put into national advertising.

Considerable and consistent attention was always given to point-of-sale promotion. Free product trays, traffic builders, related products, etc. were regularly offered to the public as an inducement to buy Oneida stainless. Such promotion and product was tastefully done so that it did not detract from the attention to or image of O. L.'s stainless.

In the 1950s, corporate identification was just beginning to be stressed rather than brand names (except for packaged goods). The theory was that the corporation goes on forever (presumably) whereas brands and trademarks may come and go. At about this time, Oneida began to develop its stainless lines which were considered pretty declassé by those who sold products with the Community trademark. Bob Landon mentioned how, at a Community Plate sales meeting, the salesmen were told stainless was a metal made for sewer pipes!

Thus, the early lines of stainless were relegated to backstamps that said Oneidacraft Deluxe and Oneidacraft Premier. And, as things turned out, this turn of events played directly into promotion of the corporate name to the consuming public. "Community" was left with a dying product and a dying promotional concept, while "Oneida" became the umbrella beneath which all product eventually was promoted.

Adding significant factory volume with consequent opportunity to lower unit costs and learn new manufacturing techniques, Special Sales under George "Carload" Kramer drummed up some early stainless business. In the mid-1950s, a Lever Bros. promotion moved several million units of product and, though bid below full cost, returned enough profit so that (legend has it) Oneida gave some money back to Lever.

Kramer's low-quality order of conventionally made product taught nothing new technologically. Oneida did learn, however, that money could be made with stainless. That clarified things for Dunc Robertson who worried that fewer manufacturing operations meant less opportunity to add value to stainless as compared to plate.

During the period the company was still wedded to silverplate and keeping the "Community" name from being tarnished by contact with stainless flatware, various customers such as Stanley Home Products and General Mills were beginning to inquire about stainless availability from Oneida. In 1958, Kramer set up a dealer loader promotion with AC Spark Plug involving about 30,000 gross of Oneidacraft Deluxe product.

Whether O. L. wanted to keep the Community trademark sanitized or not, when General Mills was nearing the end of its consumer premium contract for silverplate (*Queen Bess*), it was agreed that their new stainless line would be backstamped "Oneida Community Stainless." Apparently, this was accomplished on the spot by General Mills with the approval of Dunc Robertson and the O. L. executive committee. The first stainless pattern made for "The General" was *Twin Star* which was followed two years later, in 1963, by *My Rose*—an enormously successful pattern which stayed active until 1977. When launched, *My Rose* was expected to pull fewer than 400,000 place settings from its initial advertising. In fact, it pulled over 600,000.

Finally, it should be emphasized that Dunc Robertson organized the Stainless Steel Manufacturers Association to fight the flood of Japanese imports. This effort was successful to the point that Oneida was able to focus on competitive efforts against domestic makers such as Ekco, International, Wallace and National Silver. Ekco had been an early leader in stainless flatware but withdrew after Oneida got rolling and the other organizations never did catch up with Oneida's multi-faceted program.

Someone at International Silver was heard to say that he hoped Oneida would sell a lot of *Chateau* at its then current price as O. L. would go broke in the process. Pete Noyes liked to relate how, in the mid-1960s, some competitors had gotten into O. L.'s sales suite at a closed sales exposition. Since they were already there, Pete showed them the new pattern and said something like, "Not bad for $39.95." One of the competitors said O. L.'s retail price was more like his cost price. As the decade of the 1960s wore on, O. L.'s sales lead and product development continued to increase. Domestic competition continued to wither and finally more or less ceased with International's attempt in the early 1970s to send a spy into the Oneida factory to see how we did things.

If value is the sum total of such tangible things as quality, availability and design and such intangibles as name, image and advertising versus the price charged, then by the mid-sixties, Oneida was well ahead of the field. Given the sales volume generated by the total program and the improvements in production efficiency made by the factory, O. L.'s unit costs were the lowest in the domestic industry. Also, its retail prices were the lowest and its gross profits the highest.

In sum, I do not think a corporate decision was ever made to shift the company's focus from silverplate to stainless. Rather, it was a gradual process as the consumer drifted away from plate to a more carefree product—stainless. Once this drift gathered momentum, with stainless sales gaining and silverplate resuscitation attempts unavailing, more and more corporate resources were put behind stainless. Gradually seeing economic salvation in stainless, it was natural for management to encourage these trends as the 1950s progressed. Fortunately for Oneida, the right ingredients came together at the right time:

- Young sales management, working the market ahead of traditional competition, came up with a new way to distribute a new product.
- A talented engineering department developed innovative ways to make a better product at less cost from a new material.
- Excellent designers brought new thinking to stainless design.
- An innovative advertising campaign placed stainless teaspoon "samples" in consumer hands where their beauty could be appreciated.
- Novel department store displays delivered good profits along with the excellent price/value for new markets.
- Collateral development of special sales markets abetted both lower costs and manufacturing innovation.

Thus, from modest beginnings a stainless program evolved step by step. Oneida seemed to have the people needed to develop the programs necessary to exploit evolving opportunities. Thanks to them, a fully developed capacity to make and market stainless happened earlier at Oneida than elsewhere in the country.

Note to Chapter 3

1   This chapter is drawn from an Oneida Ltd. memorandum written and circulated by author in 1994 and in the author's possession.

4 | Pierrepont T. Noyes, 1960-1981

Pete Noyes, 1970

It came as no surprise when Pierrepont T. "Pete" Noyes became president in 1960. On February 1, 1955, a series of executive rearrangements occurred with Noyes becoming Executive Vice President and General Manager. A new lineup of executive vice-presidents then looked like this: Hamilton Allen—Manufacturing, Richard Bloom—Sales, and Robert Wayland-Smith—Finance. Each of these people had had years of experience with the company. Robertson remained as president of the corporation and in announcing the promotions had this to say: "As president of the company, I still remain as its chief executive officer, but others are going to do all the work."[1] When 1960 rolled around, Robertson was 79 years old and still vigorous as Chairman of the Board, although no longer President.

P. T. Noyes was the son of P. B. Noyes and had, from his youth, thoroughly internalized everything Oneida—the company's values, development, and operations. Graduating from Colgate University in 1936, he had married and joined the company in the same year. After initial training, he was installed as a salesman based in Ohio, then moved to other territories and returned to Oneida when World War II commenced. During the war, he was involved with the production of various war materials and once the war concluded was back in sales as an assistant sales manager. In 1946, he was elected to the board of directors and to the executive committee in 1951.

Pete had a warm and welcoming manner. He was genuinely interested in people and had no reason to think that his charm would not prevail anytime it was needed. The Oneida Ltd. personnel department once screened each employee with a standard test—the Aptitude Vector Analysis. Noyes said that he showed up with a "charm pattern." This characteristic would come in very handy on many occasions. For example, a West Coast investor once purchased a substantial amount of Oneida's common stock. Not much was known about the person or what his ambitions were for the stock. Noyes made it a point to visit him, tell him about the company, and soon had the investor's endorsement and enthusiastic advice.

By nature, energetic and optimistic, he was a great motivator giving confidence to both individuals and the corporation at large. He passed his enthusiasm along to employees at all levels and to customers whom he visited during his frequent travels. Along with all this, he would sometimes move eclectically on situations he didn't fully understand and act without consulting those who had been working on the problem. Sometimes "school would not keep" and, without explanation, he would fail to appear at a meeting or appointment anticipated by an employee. To a certain extent, Noyes dealt in ambiguity, not liking things and expectations to be so tightly defined that they might decrease his room to maneuver. He liked to say, "Yes" to everybody, a particularly appealing and welcoming quality. As one Northern Ireland executive said, "Noyes wants everyone to be nice friends and get along." One thing he did not want to do, by his own admission, was to fire people, and he seldom had to. It was an approach that could be confusing but, for the most part, it worked.

When Noyes became President, he had behind him a set of seasoned executives whose professional capacity, character, and understanding of the company's values and way of operating ran deep. They could be called on to do the right things in the right way and to shore up any gaps Noyes might have left lying around. This would not always be the case. Later on when this group of original cohorts began to retire and were replaced from the talents on hand, the company would experience a change in the way things were done and in the prevailing atmospherics under which they were done.

Sherrill, 1940's

The Oneida Ltd. factory complex in Sherrill, early 1950's

As he moved into the head position in 1960, Noyes found himself presiding over the first annual loss the company had suffered since the early 1930s. It came to an after-tax deficit of over $498,000 and represented a down-turn of about $1,000,000 from the previous year's profit. Various events conspired to bring about this poor result. According to the annual report, silverplate sales were still down, sterling silver was also well below expectations despite a new pattern introduction, and the new melamine dinnerware line showed heavy losses. Thus, sales of the most profitable lines were hurt severely. The dinnerware line registered increased start-up costs while encountering extreme price competition due to overcapacity in the industry. While the Canadian division had made a little money, the new factory development in Northern Ireland had required large capital expenditures.

However, some good things were happening. Silverplated holloware showed signs of coming to life with a range of new items and lines. Most importantly for the present and future, Noyes could report that stainless steel flatware "has been the rapidly growing product in our industry. It is now our major product line with a satisfactory gross profit."[2] Although his first year as president did not look good from a profit point of view, things would soon improve in most sales areas. Further, important developments in stainless steel flatware would soon introduce a new era of corporate prosperity.

Noyes' second year witnessed a considerable turnaround. The annual report for fiscal 1961 showed profit, before tax, of almost $750,000 versus the over $900,000 loss before taxes in 1960. Sales were better than expected in silverplate. Sterling silver sales were up along with those of plated holloware. Melamine dinnerware, however, was still problematic. However, stainless steel featured marketing results that "were most satisfactory despite intensified domestic competition," with sizeable foreign imports "stabilized below their former savagely harmful high rate." The tariff quota was back in place and the Japanese had voluntarily regulated their exports to the U. S. Noyes expected this overall "good trend" to continue. He attributed it partly to cutting severe overhead expense and to tightening controls.

Yet, dividends were decreased and that caused some dispersal of local stock ownership. Over several years, the common stock dividend had sunk from $1.25 a share in 1955 to 50 cents in 1961. Noyes was concerned about the dividend cut. Although an increased dividend had not been "earned" by operating results, it was nonetheless affordable given the company's strong financial position which featured reserves of almost $4,500,000 in cash or cash equivalents. Current assets were four times greater than current liabilities and there was no long-term debt. Total current assets at $12,365,000 were $10,862,434 in excess of current liabilities.[3] In sum, the future was looking better and better. The next year would witness a new style of annual report with more complete and exact sales data.

The decade of the 1960s saw Oneida emerge as the clear leader in the growth area of the tableware industry—stainless steel flatware. As the nation prospered during that era, so did Oneida. Over those years, company sales advanced by approximately 180%, net income by 390%, and the common stock dividend by 415%. By the mid-1960s, Oneida's unit volume had increased by 67% and employment totaled 3,173 people. That was up from 2,576 at the start of the decade and, needless to say, annual bonuses were being paid.[4]

Other products did not fare so well. Silverplate sales continued to struggle against the rise of stainless flatware. Holloware volume was up due to the introduction of new and varied lines and items but profits were dubious. Sterling flatware went into a decline and melamine dinnerware remained, at best, marginally profitable. Also, long-term debt went from being non-existent in 1961 to $14,889,300 by 1970 as capital expenditures tried to keep manufacturing capability up to the demand for stainless flatware.[5]

During the 1960s, Oneida imported and sold some cutlery and low-quality stainless made abroad by others. Gold plate was produced in Oneida's factory primarily for Special Sales (i.e., non-regular retail) purposes. A new factory came on line in Mexico to serve that and other Latin American markets with inexpensive stainless flatware.

One startling development was an attempted takeover of the company by a wire manufacturer from Brooklyn. This individual who had accumulated some Oneida stock was soundly trounced by stockholders loyal to company tradition at the annual meeting in 1965. However, he did shake up Oneida management who were moved to put three non-employees on the board of directors. This, in turn, prompted a 1-for-4 stock split and the decision to list the company, in 1966, on the New York Stock Exchange.

Overall, the most important corporate event of the 1960s was growth of stainless steel. As that decade ended, Oneida was on a roll which would carry it in good fortune for a number of years. Even the factory was making goods below standard cost now and again—a rare development given the traditional attempt by cost accountants to make manufacturing efficiency stretch by lowering standard costs. The 1970s saw continued development and increased market share by Oneida's stainless steel flatware. Substantial year to year corporate sales increases were common despite the drag of such traditional products as silverplate and sterling.

As the 1970s progressed a number of diverse events occurred. An observation tower for Niagara Falls tourists, built on the lawn of the Canadian factory in 1964, was sold in 1972 along with the handsome stone factory behind it. An emblematic jewelry firm located in Attleboro, Massachusetts, was purchased in 1973 for $1,500,000 and a new knife plant built at Oneida. A new Canadian factory began operation in 1974.

Melamine dinnerware was liquidated the same year and its equipment was successfully disposed of. A new business development division was set up to sell into the huge, nationwide giftware market.

Magazine ad for Oneida Ltd.

ONEIDA (COMMUNITY) LIMITED

7—ONEIDA DAILY DISPATCH, Saturday, Sept. 1, 1972

PIERREPONT T. NOYES —
President and Chairman of the Board

A LABOR DAY MESSAGE FROM ONEIDA SILVERSMITHS

"A lot of things about the way we do business have changed in the last 125 years, but the most important one hasn't ...putting people first'.'

That's what the people who pioneered this community had in mind when they first got together. It's an idea that started with them—and seems to have stayed with us. Just putting people first.

That's why we keep on reaching for a quality of life where people can work and live in common respect. And that's where the value of work comes in.

You see, our jobs do carry respect and dignity. For most of us, in fact, work is still a privilege. And no matter what that work is, it contributes to making our area something special...a place where living is the way people want it to be.

Maybe that's why the people who work with us give so much of themselves day after day to make our success possible. And, of course, they ought to share in it.

We try to make sure they do. Take job security that's something pretty important to everyone. At Oneida, we've been fortunate to maintain a relatively steady level of employment despite the heavy import competition of the last few years. This, along with our wage level, employee benefits,and working environment is a combination that's hard to beat.

Combination—that's the point. Certainly, somebody can always outdo us in some way. But not on the whole. Not on the combination that makes our quality of life what it is. And, believe me, we intend to keep improving on it as we go along. . . for everybody.

Oneida Silversmiths . . . putting People First

Labor Day Ad, 1972

At mid-point in 1975, a recession year, the company experienced a rare downturn in sales. Long-term debt stood at close to $17,000,000 and cash/cash equivalents exceeded current liabilities by more than 19%.[6] The company, however, was highly liquid and capable of financing both future needs and occasional setbacks. Importantly, John L. Marcellus had been promoted from his position as Vice President and General Manager to Executive Vice President and General Manager in 1975

Things were looking up in 1976 with the purchase of the Camden Wire Company on whose board Pete Noyes had served many years. With the premature death of its principal owner, Camden shareholders were amenable to seeing the company locally owned. Having been built step-by-step in solid fashion over a number of years, it was a business that set the standard for quality and reliability among producers of non-insulated copper wire. Camden had excellent management willing to carry on, an over 30% yearly return on assets, and a positive cash flow. From Oneida's point of view, acquisition of this highly profitable industrial products company would substantially broaden Oneida's sales and income basis. And, at $14,000,000, the purchase was a bargain which would pay Oneida Ltd. dividends for many years.[7] With the end of the tariff quota which had offered some import protection to Oneida's manufacture of stainless flatware (1976), this acquisition could not have been more timely.

Pete Noyes and Jim Colway, late 1970's

In 1977, the tableware business was sluggish with slow sales in the first half of the year followed by problems with manufacturing efficiency. Thanks to Camden, however, 1977 was a boom year for Oneida Ltd.— "the best earnings per share in your company's history," Noyes related cheerfully. Corporate sales were up by $55,500,000 and earnings per share increased by 52%. Shareholders were rewarded with a five-for-four stock split. Stockholder equity was 34% greater than long-term debt. Although cash was down drastically, the company could still cover its current liabilities with only cash and cash equivalent current assets. It is interesting to note that tableware sales of about $100,500,000 provided somewhat over $7,000,000 in operating profits while Camden sales of $50,500,000 turned in operating profits of nearly $6,000,000.[8]

Another acquisition about the time of Camden Wire was a two-engine turboprop airplane which seated about eight people including the pilot. It was very useful for short trips to places difficult to reach, or alternatively, to busy airports within a few hundred miles from which connections for further travel could be made in timely fashion. The convenience of this plane soon led to the purchase of a larger, long-range, pre-owned jet and to the hiring of a second pilot. When this aircraft showed its age (a problem with pressurization being one of them), the company signed a lease on a new French-made jet. This plane made many long-haul trips and was eventually shut down by subsequent management as an economy measure. Perhaps the company should have stayed with the first plane.

A seminal event occurred in February 1977 when Noyes orchestrated a profound change in the size and composition of the board of directors. Since post-Oneida Community days, the company had been managed by a board composed largely of employees. As time passed, managers of major departments were appointed to this board so that, by 1977, there were twenty-two members including the three outside individuals who had been brought in following the 1960s takeover attempt. A six-person executive committee looked after the day-to-day management, but the full board met once a month to review corporate financial results, plans, progress, and problems as well as to pass any resolutions requiring board action.

On that day in early 1977, directors received a notice to attend a special meeting of the board. No agenda was supplied for the occasion nor was its purpose made known in advance. The meeting was to be held in the basement mailroom of the Administrative Building because the board room was being re-carpeted. When it opened, it soon became apparent that the purpose of the meeting was to have board members vote themselves out of existence so that a new and smaller board could be nominated. This was to be done immediately so that the new board could be listed in the upcoming annual report which was urgently required at the printers.

The meeting, therefore, resembled an ambush more than a deliberative session. After some vague talk by an outside board member (Lawrence Appley) about how the new set-up would aid corporate planning, another official (William Matthews, subject of an upcoming chapter) called for a voice vote to end the existence of the old board.

Those in on the secret were the members of the executive committee and the trio of outside directors. The twelve shocked board members who were in the dark went along with the proceedings, presumably out of trust in the judgment of the remaining directors. No one asked why time for deliberation had not been allowed, and why the whole matter was handled in such a non-traditional, non-consultative manner. Upon reflection, it represented a watershed in how the company would manage and communicate.

1978 was another momentous year featuring two events that would have long-lasting impact on Oneida Ltd. J. L. Marcellus was moved up to President and Chief Operating Officer with Pete Noyes becoming Chairman of the Board and remaining the Chief Executive Officer. Next, the company decided to buy Rena-Ware Distributors, a long-time customer that sold stainless steel cookware direct to consumers, mostly in overseas markets. It had annual sales of nearly $70 million at time of purchase and net income of $5.5 million. It cost Oneida Ltd. $24.1 million. While this acquisition had a promising beginning, it later ended up badly for both companies.

Sales rose 22% at that time. Earnings per share gained over 37% and a five-for-four stock split was announced. New buildings were put up in Camden and at Oneida. Some management "restructuring" was put in place affecting planning and subsidiary management. Results from Rena-Ware figured into only two months of the year. Noyes, however, was ecstatic about the new member of the Oneida family, saying in his annual report letter for fiscal year 1979, "the relationship [with Rena-Ware] is just as fine as we hoped. Actually finer!"[9]

The good news continued in fiscal 1980 with all parts of the corporation experiencing good fortune. Oneida Canada Ltd. had been producing astounding operating income results. The Mexican operation was being enlarged as the national economy boomed. Oneida, UK was still struggling but hopeful. Camden was a major producer of earnings despite erratic copper prices, and Rena-Ware had acquired "Miracle Maid," a direct-to-the-consumer seller of cookware in the U. S. Since this partially offset that company's dependence on foreign sales, Noyes reported with satisfaction that Rena-Ware "is experiencing healthy growth in sales volume this year, and indications are they will be a strong earner in 1980." With it all, the corporation remained in good financial shape with an improved equity-to-debt ratio and plenty of coverage for current liabilities. Operating income was over 10% and net income nearly 5% of sales—both important financial benchmarks showing improvement.[10]

"No one makes a big profit on the business of Oneida Ltd.," the *Washington Post* reported from an interview with Noyes in 1976. "The guiding management philosophy always has been to pay high wages [to workers] and relatively low salaries [to the managers]."[11] This policy, put in place by Noyes' father and maintained by his son-in-law, Dunc Robertson, began to change as the 1970s wore on. Some impetus to change may have resulted from the discovery that a straight commission salesman at Leavens Manufacturing, the company's emblematic jewelry affiliate, was making more than Noyes. In any event, Noyes' salary went from $65,000 in 1970 to $301,000 by 1980.

Pete Noyes' final full year on the job would be 1980 and, in his last letter to shareholders, he reported "record earnings of over $22,000,000, reflecting a 47% gain over 1979." Sales were up 19% "to a record level of around $360,000,000." Another five-for-four stock split was declared and management was said to be "ever sharper." Rena-Ware, at this point, "had a fine year" and was "looking forward to continued growth," with 14,000 independent contractor agents up from 9,000 when purchased by Oneida. Oneida, as company auditors stated, remained in a strong financial position: "The present level of indebtedness combined with the credit resources that are available, places the company in a position to finance a continuation of the growth experienced in the current year and to take advantage of additional opportunities that may become available."[12]

Noyes could look back over a decade that had seen corporate sales rise from $72,628,665 in 1972 to $359,590,640 in fiscal year 1981 with sales roughly balanced among stainless flatware, industrial wire, and cookware. Net income went from $2,247,512 to $22,518,395 during this period, retained earnings from $21,412,766 to $44,143,317, fixed assets from $36,310,303 to $66,770,910, and long-term debt from $13,891,900 to $40,543,593. Stockholders equity began at $31,519,632 and ended at $89,570,478 with several stock splits along the way.[13] In keeping with its historically conservative financial practice, the company had current liquid assets (cash and receivables) well in excess of current liabilities. It was truly a picture that showed great and diverse progress and promise. And, it was a picture that was to drastically and dreadfully change. With Pete Noyes' departure, an era would come to a close.

In the spring of 1981, Noyes—67 years old and two years past the normal retirement age—suffered a stroke which left him partially paralyzed. He resigned as president later that year following a visit by two directors conveying the board's wish that he retire and become Honorary Chairman of the Board. This development upset him because he supposed, unrealistically, that he would continue as CEO despite his disability. When asked later how he had intended to retire, he said that he had in mind to simply walk in one day, clear a few things out of his desk, and leave. In the event, Noyes maintained an office in the administration building until his death in 1992. He appeared there more-or-less daily during these intervening years, available for advice or conversation. He also participated in board meetings and took particular interest in the 1989 corporate divestment of the Mansion House, his family's ancestral home.

Despite the physical disability preventing him from doing what he loved—skiing, fishing, training horses, Noyes displayed a grit and determination to prevail over his limitations surprising to those who saw him chiefly as a fun-loving person. His well-attended memorial service was held in the Big Hall of the Mansion House where he had presided over so many annual meetings.

In the year following his death, Oneida Ltd. employees, on their own initiative, erected a memorial to Noyes which was placed at the factory entrance. It says, in part—"To employees he was just 'Pete'—a friend who identified with all workers as eagerly as he helped Oneida become the world's largest tableware company. His charm, spirit and vision will never be forgotten." The later sale of the factory by Oneida Ltd. would see this memorial find a new home at the Oneida Community Golf Course where he had played so well for so many years. It stands, at this writing, as a reminder to those who knew him, knew what he represented, or, perhaps, as an intriguing curiosity to those who knew him not and wished they had.

Notes to Chapter 4

1 Quoted from "Pierrepont T. Noyes Will Become General Manager," *Oneida Daily Dispatch*, January 26, 1955.
2 Oneida Ltd. Annual Report for Fiscal Year Ended January 31, 1961.
3 Oneida Ltd. Annual Report for Fiscal Year Ended January 31, 1962.
4 Oneida Ltd. Annual Report for Fiscal Years Ended January 31, 1969; 16, and January 31, 1966.
5 Oneida Ltd. Annual Report for Fiscal Year Ending January 30, 1971.
6 Oneida Ltd. Annual Report for Fiscal Year Ended January 31, 1976.
7 Oneida Ltd. Annual Report for Fiscal Year Ended January 29, 1977.
8 Oneida Ltd. Annual Report for Fiscal Year Ended January 28, 1978.
9 Oneida Ltd. Annual Report for Fiscal Year Ended January 27, 1979.
10 Oneida Ltd. Annual Report for Fiscal Year Ended January 26, 1980.

11 "Oneida: Experiment Dies, but the Company Thrives," *Washington Post*, August 22, 1976.
12 Oneida Ltd. Annual Report for Fiscal Year Ended January 31, 1981, 26.
13 Oneida Ltd. Annual Report for Fiscal Year Ended January 31, 1981, 28-29.

5 | John L. Marcellus, 1981-1986

John Marcellus, 1981

John Marcellus' reign as corporate president was brief but memorable in many ways. A native of Clinton, N. Y., he graduated from Syracuse University in 1942, Cum Laude, amidst a small group of business majors. An imposing figure well over six feet in height, he looked the part of a president. Added to this was a strong inclination for self-assertion which made his presence easily noticed.

After joining the company in 1946, he served as what Pete Noyes called a marginal salesman in the Cleveland, Ohio, area for some years. His superiors wanted him out of selling and Les Smith (Domestic Sales) once said that the company had been looking for a home office marketing job for him. Accordingly, when a short-lived arrangement as a flatware market manager came about in the late 1960s, John was called in to fill it. After a relatively brief period of time, the market manager concept was abandoned in favor of a return to product managers and Marcellus soon became head of product operations over more experienced personnel. A later article in *Forbes* magazine stated, inaccurately, that he had run "virtually every department in the company during his 36-year career."[1]

To better coordinate incoming orders with factory scheduling, regular "inventory" meetings were set up at the Administrative Building in the 1970s. These, in my memory, became a platform for Marcellus to assert himself and belabor factory management.

Equally dominant in these meetings was the head of manufacturing, Herb Stoughton. He had been hired from Detroit by Oneida's Canastota affiliate in the early 1950s as a labor negotiator. Sales management stood somewhat in awe of Herb because he was strong-minded, equipped with a detailed understanding of production, and ready to defend his ideas. It was natural therefore that he and Marcellus should clash.

Marcellus' star began to rise not long after the start of these inventory meetings. He became Vice President and General Manager in 1974 and Executive Vice President and General Manager in 1975 at which point he was widely seen as Pete Noyes' successor. In 1978, Marcellus was named President and Chief Operating Officer and, finally, Chairman of the Board, President and Chief Executive Officer following Noyes' stroke in the spring of 1981. Years later, when asked if he installed Marcellus as his successor to fight with Herb Stoughton for him, Pete Noyes told me, "Something like that." For his part, Marcellus later stated that at the time he was made General Manager, he "had the initial approval of all of Oneida's executive committee members but one, specifically, Mr. Stoughton."[2]

The Marcellus management style represented radical change from the familiar in several respects. For one thing, he was terrible at delivering formal sentiments to an audience. At large gatherings, such as the annual shareholders meeting in the Mansion House or even less formal occasions like the Silver Niblick golf outing, his inadequacy as a public speaker was painful to witness.

In smaller business contexts, furthermore, Marcellus set a tone at odds with the easy-going way Pete Noyes led and motivated the corporation. Although John could be low-key and reasonable in private one-on-one sessions, the management level meetings he conducted often were filled with self-drama, reminders of his exalted position, reference to himself in the third person, denigration of people not present, and loud tones of voice. It tended to silence meeting attendees whose ideas differed from his. Most present knew his position on a subject generally before discussion began and also those people of whom he approved or disapproved. There was a well known "A" team and "B" team of company executives.

This approach was questioned publicly on one occasion. At an American management seminar in Hamilton, N. Y., Larry Appley, Oneida board member and guru of the American Management Association, described how a leader should conduct a meeting. The issue should be stated to begin with and then each attendee asked to give his ideas and opinions as to how the matter should be resolved. The leader should keep his own opinion to himself if he wants others to speak freely. When the meeting is concluded, the leader may or may not have modified his opinion and decision based on what he has heard from his subordinates. Marcellus listened to all this and then said, in effect, "You may believe that stuff, Larry, but I don't. When I've studied the subject, I've got it right and I make the decision." Appley, shaking his head, rejoined, "Then you will never hear from them." One person at the seminar tried to cover for John saying, "Mr. Appley, don't you think when you have strong leadership, there is no room for management by committee?" At the close of the meeting, Marcellus, upon reflection, did say that from then on the company was going to be run along the lines Appley described. Regardless, this session laid out the corporate management problem in very stark terms for which most attendees were grateful even if no change in management style occurred.

It was, perhaps, John's misfortune to become corporate head just as Rena-Ware sales and profits were set to decline. The first two years of this acquisition had seen it make major contributions to corporate sales and operating profits. In 1981, its figures headed down and continued to do so. From a high point of nearly $128,000,000 in 1981, sales declined to about $103,000,000 by 1983. During this time cookware operating profits went from about $15,000,000 to $8,000,000. Over its brief span of Oneida ownership, various surprises occurred having to do with currency, inventory devaluations, and foreign lawsuits, among other things. Rena-Ware was simply a business that Oneida never understood despite years of association with it as a supplier of exclusive flatware patterns before its acquisition, and after thousands of miles of travel by corporate jet back and forth to the state of Washington where it was headquartered.

In 1983, Rena-Ware was sold back to the people from whom it was purchased at a substantial loss for Oneida. The annual report for 1986 would show a loss of over $14,000,000 for the Rena-Ware adventure.[3]

A few smaller acquisitions had taken place in the early 1980s. Webster-Wilcox, a famous hollowware trademark was purchased from the company's traditional tableware rival, International Silver (Insilco) for $2,600,000. An article in a trade magazine of the time reported that Webster-Wilcox had long been unprofitable for International Silver because of a weak economy, high silver prices, and foreign competition.[4] Oneida sent personnel to Meriden, Connecticut, to attend to packing existing inventory and tools for shipment to its Sherrill factory. As it happened, Oneida produced little Webster-Wilcox product, found many of the dies and tools defective and worn and, via its company store, managed to sell off existing inventories of the high quality product it had acquired.

Also in 1981, the Wiggin Group in the United Kingdom was purchased for $673,000, thus bringing to the company the well known Old Hall Stainless Hollowware line (plus an excellent flatware pattern), Bridge Crystal, and Wiggin chains. Of this aggregation, all were eventually disposed of except for the flatware pattern which was added to the company's U. K. flatware portfolio. Factory expansion in Mexico and at Camden Wire occurred and, overall, a total of $13,000,000 was spent on these affiliates. Various management initiatives were afoot, among them a "Planning Action Group," which was a manpower review committee, and a group to examine long-range financial requirements.

One of Marcellus' projects was the refurbishment of the Administration Building over the course of two years. Accomplished without benefit of an architect, its cost may have been in the neighborhood of $9,000,000. The basic idea was to provide more air-conditioned work space and privacy without having to enlarge the building. As it turned out, the additional space transformed the main floor into a rabbit warren of individual office cubicles. Another elevator was installed, but one that did nothing more than travel between two floors. The former large and flexible sales conference room was converted into a tiered auditorium with limited-seating capacity and display accommodation. In times past, a wide range of employees had the opportunity to see, understand and applaud the immediate plans for expanding tableware sales. Now, attendance at sales meetings would be severely restricted.[5]

Of substantial note was the failure of the Stainless Steel Manufacturer's Association to secure tariff increases from the International Trade Commission in 1984. Two companies not only bailed out of the association before the hearing but turned actively against such tariff increases. The Commission ruled that Far Eastern imports were not seriously injuring U. S. manufacturers. As Oneida had experienced several years of good profits and represented 95% of domestic production, it was easy to turn down the case. It also came out that Oneida itself was a major importer of cheap stainless flatware as its own production of such merchandise had skyrocketed over the past ten years. Marcellus was correct in warning of "mass inroads from the new supplier, China," as time would soon enough tell.[6]

The acquisition of Buffalo China in 1983 for $17,500,000 put the company firmly in the hotel and catering dinnerware business. This carefully managed company was the largest domestic supplier, in unit volume, of heavy, low-end product. It had made significant investments in technological upgrading and had plans to produce higher quality dinnerware. And, it made product below standard cost—a novelty as far as Oneida Ltd. was concerned.

In 1984, Leavens, the emblematic jewelry maker, was sold for $3,100,000. It had been purchased in 1973 for $1,500,000 which netted down to $1,000,000 once its accumulation of cash and the sale of gold product samples were taken into consideration. Its primitive accounting system allowed it to show outstanding paper profits as the price of gold rose in the 1970s. The reverse had come true in 1981 when the price of gold went from $800 an ounce to $400. Leavens always maintained a positive cash flow. The same year, DJ Distributors, a Canadian-based importer of outsized stainless flatware for the catering trade was purchased for $3,250,000.[7]

There was some important management shuffling. In 1983, Bob Sanderson became Vice Chairman of the corporate board having been President of the Oneida Silversmith Division. Wendell Wild then moved from Vice President to President of this division. By the autumn of 1985, both had resigned or retired along with Jim Colway, long-time head of advertising and sales promotion. Colway, in association with the company's advertising agency, had done an outstanding job of putting the Oneida name prominently in the mind of the tableware consumer.

The April 1985 proxy statement revealed a new and substantial benefit awarded to top executives. Senior officers retiring at age 62 would now receive, at age 65, 45% and 50% of their average annual compensation. The new supplemental retirement plan (SERP) was described as "non-qualified, non-contributory and unfunded."[8] This line and some other verbiage disappeared with the 1993 proxy statement. Subsequently, no mention at all was made of how SERP was funded and, by the time of the 1999 proxy statement, SERP itself apparently had disappeared from the public record. However, the next year's proxy statement revealed a new "Restoration Plan" under which a few top officials would receive at least 40% of their average annual compensation.[9]

Capital investments had continued through the first half of the 1980s with particular reference to Camden Wire which purchased and then expanded a factory building in Arkansas. Additionally, an extensive and expensive program to modernize manufacturing processes at Camden's home factory was undertaken. Tableware sales remained difficult with gross profits sinking marginally and import competition heating up. Overall, net income of $22,518,000 had declined 56% from fiscal 1981—Pete Noyes' last year as president—to $9,909,000 in fiscal 1985.[10]

When losses developed during the second quarter of 1986, the outside directors (except for two who were not let in on the plot), in conjunction with all inside directors, decided that Marcellus' services were no longer required. A plan for this kind of cabal had been mooted since the early 1980s and had reached the retired Pete Noyes who took it up with an outside director. At that time, business was not bad enough to warrant such action. However, by July 1986, that was precisely the case. Marcellus was summoned from his Adirondack camp to a meeting in Syracuse where he received the news of his resignation at the request of the board of directors. Oneida's Director of Public Relations was quoted as saying, "After more than 40 years, it was decided it was time for Mr. Marcellus to retire."[11]

By his own lights, John Marcellus had tried to provide what he saw as strong management and to seize what he saw as business opportunities. I thought his abrasive style was not what was needed and his choice of confidantes was not highly regarded by management at large—not "OCQ," as was once said. A retired director who visited the factory following the announcement of Marcellus' resignation said that he'd never seen so many people with so many smiles whose dividends had just been cut.

As for the company, the balance sheet had taken a turn for the worse. Cash and receivables had exceeded total current liabilities by $22,900,000 in Pete Noyes' final year, fiscal 1981. In 1986, current liabilities were in excess of current cash and receivables by over $7,400,000, a negative swing of over $30,000,000. Nonetheless, Marcellus maintained a firm grip on long-term debt with stockholder equity in excess of long-term debt by over 100% in his full final year. Although the company had negative cash flow for fiscal year 1986, its overall financials were not in bad shape. Its products were well-placed and well-accepted by the public. Consumer advertising had been maintained and capital expenditures were adequate.[12]

Excluding fiscal year 1984 when the Rena-Ware divestiture loss was booked, fiscal year 1987, which saw Marcellus' departure at mid-point, recorded the first net income loss since Pete Noyes' first year as president—1961. A loss of $7,258,000 was enhanced by "Big Bath" accounting as the new management team wrote down or off any dubious assets in order to clear the decks for dramatic financial recovery.[13]

Under Marcellus, an actuary dedicated to setting up the previously mentioned Supplemental Retirement Plan had been hired. However, disappointed Marcellus may have been to be nudged out by directors just rewarded with handsome retirement payouts, he himself was a primary beneficiary who could look forward to a very prosperous old age.

Notes to Chapter 5

1 "Resetting the clock in Oneida," Paul B. Brown, *Forbes*, February 1, 1982, 85, 89.
2 Deposition of John L. Marcellus, Jr., June 17-18, 1986, in "Peter Tartarian v. Oneida Ltd., et al.," 3 (5-page typescript of an action brought by an official of Leavens Manufacturing in the author's possession).
3 Oneida Ltd. Annual Report for Fiscal Years Ended January 31, 1981, 20; January 29, 1983, 22; and January 25, 1986, 23.
4 "International Silver Shuts Webster-Wilcox," *Retailing Home Furnishings*, March 2, 1981.
5 Nick Vanderwall, personal communication; Oneida Ltd. Annual Report for Fiscal Years Ended January 30, 1982 and January 29, 1983, 32.
6 "Importers counter Oneida," Richard Wightman, *hfs—The Weekly Home Furnishings Newspaper*, April 9, 1984, Section 1.

7   Oneida Ltd. Annual Reports for Fiscal Years Ended January 28, 1984, 17, and January 26, 1985, 23.
8   Oneida Ltd. Annual Report for Fiscal Year Ended January 29, 1983; Oneida Ltd. Proxy Statement, May 25, 1985 (6); "Bob Sanderson and Wendell Wild Retire," *The Oneida Silversmith*, Fall-Winter 1985.
9   Oneida Ltd. Proxy Statements, April 23, 1999 and May 31, 2000, 9.
10 Oneida Ltd. Annual Report for Fiscal Year Ended January 26, 1985, 39.
11 "2 chosen to replace Oneida Ltd. boss," Jack Durschlag, *Oneida Daily Dispatch*, July 29, 1986.
12 Oneida Ltd. Annual Report for Fiscal Year Ended January 25, 1986, 20-21.
13 Oneida Ltd. Annual Report for Fiscal Year Ended January 31, 1987, 13.

6

William D. Matthews, 1986-1999

In the summer of 1986, W. D. Matthews had been head of Oneida Ltd.'s Legal Department since the autumn of 1972 when O. E. "Ned" Cummings, the department head, died unexpectedly of a heart attack at age 52. A graduate of Union College and Cornell's law school, Matthews had joined the company in 1969 having served as an attorney with the Securities and Exchange Commission in Washington, D. C.

Along with impressing people by his energy and legal expertise, he had distinguished himself in the capture of an industrial spy set upon the company's main manufacturing plant in the spring of 1972 by Oneida Ltd.'s ancient rival, The International Silver Company (Insilco). The prototypical industrial spy of the day was described by a pulp magazine as "The man from whom no company's secrets are safe." Not so this spy. When he tried to pass himself off as a federal labor inspector, Oneida's safety manager became suspicious of the relatively safe manufacturing operations that the "inspector" was interested in. The manager terminated the factory tour, called Matthews, and gave the latter the visitor's alleged federal bona fides.

Promptly calling the appropriate Washington office to confirm this information, Matthews was told that something sounded "fishy" and that he would be called back shortly. When the call came, Matthews learned he probably had a spy on his hands. Upon calling the factory, he learned the "inspector" had left. The State Police were notified and the imposter was caught at the Utica airport. His briefcase contained a letter from an Insilco executive. The spy and his employer eventually paid fines and Oneida received a settlement from Insilco in lieu of a lawsuit. This exciting event showed how far in arrears the company's main domestic competitor knew itself to be in terms of production efficiency and capability compared to Oneida.

Matthew's predecessor, Ned Cummings, had been a member of Oneida Ltd.'s Executive Committee, a position which Matthews assumed in 1972. Thus, when he replaced Marcellus as board chairman and CEO in 1986, he had had fourteen years of exposure to company administrative practice and decision-making. It is true that he had no direct training or experience of the three main business functions: marketing, manufacturing, and finance. On the other hand, he was backed up by long-serving, capable people in manufacturing and finance.

Additionally, as corporate president and CEO, he was given Samuel J. Lanzafame, MBA, who had a background in planning, a brief tour as Managing Director of the Northern Ireland operation, and then as president of the Camden Wire affiliate. Reporting to Lanzafame were: Terry French, Lanzafame's replacement as Camden Wire president; Gary Moreau, who had limited factory experience in both staff and management positions and was put in charge of the Oneida tableware business; and Glenn Kelsey, CPA and former controller who was installed as head of the dinnerware company (Buffalo China) as well as hotel catering and international sales. Each was given the title of president and CEO of his respective area. Thus, the local newspaper could report that a planned and orderly transition was taking place upon the retirement of John Marcellus.[1]

The new management got to work by cutting the corporate dividend by 50%, a move that saved needed cash and sank the share price to somewhat over $12.00 from around $18.00. In September 1986, 45 white collar workers were fired and total employment was reduced by 200 people. The previous year, 150 management positions had been eliminated and management had taken a 10% pay cut. Reductions in 1986 cut another 15% from overhead and saved, annually, around $1,500,000. Nonetheless, the company had lost $624,000 in the first half of the year under the previous management. Far East competition was gaining, the dollar was strong, and a recession was at hand. Prospects for the full year did not look bright, new management and all. The outcome was made worse by the closing costs associated with the under-utilized factory in Northern Ireland and a $12,000,000 write-down of corporate inventory and bad debts. However, a company press release late in 1986 stated Oneida had earned $1,100,000 in the first nine months of the fiscal year.[2]

By the time accountants had finished, an ultimate loss of $7,258,000 in fiscal 1987 set the stage for an excellent upcoming fiscal year. Along with written-down inventory and overhead reduction, the company benefited from first, an appreciated Japanese yen, thus raising the price of imports, and second, the beginnings of the longest sustained domestic economic expansion of the 20th century. Things were looking up as net income hit $16,700,000 in fiscal 1988.

Fiscal year 1989 saw a continuation of overhead reduction with the elimination of the product office and a decline in the value of the heretofore strong dollar, an instigator of the "Rust Belt" during the Reagan administration. The strong dollar also contributed to labor unrest among Korean suppliers of low-cost, stainless flatware which, in turn, resulted in late shipments to anxious catering customers. It was also a year of capital expenditures totaling $18,000,000 on projects at Buffalo China, Mexico, Camden, and Oneida, along with an over $2,000,000 reduction in net income.

To generate cash as of the fourth quarter of FY 1988, $15,703,000 was taken from the employee stock option plan (ESOP) and the pension plan which was replaced by a new pension plan. This served to more than offset nearly $10,000,000 in restructuring costs involving plant closings and inventory write-offs. Camden Wire had been prospering despite facing strong price competition. Tableware was also doing well, largely because foodservice sales were robust in spite of increased expense from several causes including distribution reorganization, various new product introductions, and a number of new factory store openings.[3]

And a move had been underway to divest the Mansion House—the Oneida Community's ancestral home—to a newly formed non-profit group. This was accomplished in 1988 with Oneida Ltd. continuing to provide important in-kind and financial support for several years. Most importantly, and thanks to Matthews, the company agreed to match the first $800,000 from private donors to a "Mansion House Endowment Fund" whose proceeds were to offset customary annual operating deficits generated by the House.

The company had continued to launch new and differentiated product (gold plate on holloware) and to build more facilities for Buffalo China. Camden's new Arkansas factory was at capacity. In total, $21,000,000 had been spent in fiscal 1989 on capital projects. The year also featured two dividend increases and a 10% common stock dividend. At the late May annual meeting, Matthews was heard to say it was the company's intention to be profitable and independent and not to sell off assets or mortgage Oneida's future.[4]

In January 1989, Lanzafame resigned. He who had risen precipitously under Marcellus and who had been appointed President and COO of Oneida Ltd. by Marcellus' successor, now left abruptly to seek, it was said, new challenges.[5] Matthews took on Lanzafame's duties until December 1991, at which time Gary Moreau became corporate president and COO while still continuing to head the Oneida Silversmith division. Matthews remained as board chairman and CEO.

During much of Matthew's tenure, the company saw net income go from $7,814,000 in fiscal year 1991 to $16,972,000 in fiscal year 1997. It was an era of new ventures. Factory store expansion continued apace. New products such as upgraded enamel inlaid stainless flatware were launched along with palladium plate and acrylic "glassware." A couple of high-end retail shops were started up under the "J. Humphrey" name. (Most of these ventures were soon abandoned, not without some pain.)

Considerable optimism was expressed. *Forbes* magazine noted in 1992 that Oneida's operating income "is big enough to repay all debt in three years."[6] In the context of the global market, "Oneida is better prepared than many companies to thrive at home and abroad in this world-spanning market place," it was announced in the annual report for 1995. Oneida's competitive strategy, the same source explained, "is anchored by a commitment to an internal manufacturing network" providing "direct control over the manufacturing of many of our products" as well as a vital edge. "We have," the statement concluded, "long faced global competition."[7] Fateful words.

During the 1990s, an important consumer products wholesaler located in Georgia was purchased for $6,000,000. That meant that other wholesalers were cut off as products began to be sold direct to retailers from strategically placed company-operated warehouses. To some observers, dropping all wholesalers of consumer products seemed a strange thing to do. Obviously, if major accounts insisted on the lowest possible cost price and did not value the low inventory-fast turnover service available from wholesalers (the "LIFT" concept), the company would have had to sell them direct. Existing wholesalers could then hope for fill-in business and, in any event, could continue to look after smaller retail accounts in the secondary market. This was the distribution set-up in Canada and it had worked very well over the years. Since some distributors did not take kindly to being cut off, the company was presented with a number of law suits.

Then, in December 1995, Gary Moreau, President and COO, resigned. When he assumed those offices in 1992, his key strengths were said to be "absolute, sincere honesty."[8] Moreau apparently planned, at that time, to be at Oneida for the rest of his career. Nevertheless, he was now off to Michigan to take up the presidency of a toy firm. Matthews expressed sorrow at seeing Moreau go but perhaps he did not go far. A short time later, he turned up on the board of Libbey Glass which, shortly after that, attempted a takeover of Oneida Ltd.—a fine strategic opportunity for both companies, according to Moreau at that time.

Matthews appointed Peter J. Kallet in February of 1996 to replace Moreau. Some were surprised that he did not select Glenn Kelsey who had been made president of the foodservice (including Buffalo China) and international operations at the same time that Moreau was named president of Oneida's consumer operations. However, considerable money spent to upgrade the Buffalo factories here and in Mexico seemed to result in production costs higher than ever. That was on Kelsey's watch as was an investment in Italy to produce tableware under a new trademark, "Sant' Andrea" (not the Oneida name!), which was showing no signs of success. To Matthews, therefore, Kelsey's management record may have seemed less than stellar. On the other hand, Glenn was generally well regarded and seemed, given his time-in-grade, to be the logical choice to succeed Moreau. As a CPA and former corporate controller, he had a good understanding of the details of costs and the tableware finances. Additionally, Pete Kallet had reported to Kelsey for some years as head of foodservice sales.

The company had been wrestling with a new computerized Management Information System which permitted customers to enter orders directly to the factory and allowed closer control of production and inventories. This system, not without surprises, was in place by fiscal year 1996, a year which also proved to be the most profitable since Pete Noyes' time, 1981.

1996 featured the purchase of THC Systems Inc., better known by its dinnerware brand: Rego. A line imported from the Far East, this product had been well regarded by the former owner of Buffalo China and was an upgraded quality from Buffalo's heavy, durable offerings. The price was $46.6 million, a large part of which ($33.8 million—72%) was non-tangible "goodwill," thus starting a trend which would play out some years later.

Along with Rego came, under contract, the Rego CEO, Allan Conseur. He was to have a major part in future Oneida operations.

Kallet starting on the "goodwill" binge to disaster

At the 115th annual meeting in May 1996, Matthews advised the gathering, "that the acquisition of companies and proposed licensing agreements using the Oneida name are among the firm's long-term growth prospects."[9] Thus was proclaimed the groundwork for eventual disaster.

Camden Wire was sold in February 1997. The $59 million received for it ($43.5 million in cash) was most welcome given the purchase of Rego and funds needed for new and old ventures.[10] Once the "crown jewel" among Oneida's affiliates, Camden's profitability had fallen off due to sales declines, price competition, low copper prices, and questionable management. However, during the first five years following its acquisition in 1976, Camden had provided Oneida with exceptional cash flow, operating profits, and return on assets. It also provided Oneida with marked diversification from sole dependence on the tableware business. One can only speculate upon how wire production might have affected corporate prospects once Oneida's factory began to suffer from foreign flatware imports. Indeed, it was the prospect of low-cost electricity enjoyed by Oneida (thanks to an allocation of public power) that later influenced the Camden Wire Division of International Wire to buy half of Oneida's shut-down knife plant for wire production.

There had been times when Camden's share of net sales had been 70% of Oneida Silversmith's sales and its contribution to operating profits was 40% of Oneida's. At the same time, the wire company's Return on Assets was 32.8% to Silversmith's 20.4%. Camden's share of net sales and operating costs had vacillated for several years thanks to a sustained drop in copper prices and increased price competition. However, in the full year before Camden was sold, it produced 29% of net *corporate* sales and 15% of operating profits. Always profitable and well-established in its industry, Camden represented a very useful diversification. Previously, the virtues of diversification into industrial products had been recognized. Now, however, the presumed greater virtue of concentration on higher gross-profit consumer tableware products alone became the new corporate theme.

According to the corporation's annual report for fiscal 1997, the divestiture of Camden Wire would permit Oneida to focus "efforts on what we do best, which of course is the tableware market...We will invest the proceeds [from the sale] in our main business." And, so they did with a variety of undertakings, among them joint ventures in Australia, Italy, and Columbia and licensing agreements employing the Oneida name—a warm-up for the millennial exfoliation to shortly occur.

The stockholders letter from Matthews and Kallet in the annual report for fiscal 1997 ended with a flourish: "We have the right people in place, the right products and programs and our balance sheet is in its best position ever."[11] Despite the hyperbole, the company was then in good fiscal shape. Long-term debt was 58% of stockholder's equity. The Matthews' administration's fiscal high point was reached the next year, fiscal 1998, with net income after taxes of about 6% of net sales.

The 1997 annual report talked about "strategic moves designed to direct the company's business for years to come." The company focused on being tableware importers to achieve "a dynamic new commercial balance...for an exciting and profitable future." The proceeds from Camden Wire's sale—which were well below book value—would be used for tableware investment. But what Matthews and Kallet did not say, and may not have known, was that the company's lack of diversification doomed its future as a manufacturing entity. Shortly, it would be in the ruck battling it out with other tableware importers with the priceless Oneida name on the back of goods sold by Wal-Mart.

A major undertaking was the introduction of consumer dinnerware billed as "the largest launch since stainless flatware" and involving "500 stock-keeping units within three distinct lines of dinnerware." An $11,000,000 expansion of the Buffalo China factory was begun and $13,000,000 was laid out for an Italian design and engineering company (Sant' Andrea) that supplied the joint venture with product. Also, a 25% stake in a German crystal company was had for $9,000,000. Strong sales increases were experienced by all sales divisions with foodservice sales leading the pack with an increase of 28.4%. Company shares were at an "all time high," a 3-for-2 stock split was declared and stockholders' equity was almost double long-term debt.[12] The good times had a bit farther to roll.

The annual report for fiscal year 1998 recapitulated the good news of Oneida's significant gains for the year in net sales, income, earnings per share, and return on equity and went onto say, "We believe that the members of the Oneida Community, founded 150 years ago, would be very proud of all that our people have accomplished." Members of the Oneida Community might well have been impressed by the figures although EPS (earnings per share) and ROE (return on equity) are probably concepts unknown to them. But, what would really have astonished them was information in the proxy statement which showed Matthews receiving total compensation for the year just past of $748,578 and Kallet getting $658,718. As Bible Communists, the Perfectionists would have had a hard time reconciling such sums with their egalitarian beliefs. The same, of course, could be said of later managers of Oneida Ltd. such as P. B. Noyes and M. E. Robertson. As it turned out, the company was just four years from destruction despite all the high-priced managerial talent.[13]

Fiscal year 1999 featured, according to the annual report, a "seamless change in Oneida's leadership" with Matthews becoming Chairman of the Board in December 1998. He felt good about this, declaring that Pete Kallet was "the right man" to be his successor as Chief Executive Officer. Other Oneida executives chipped in with such praise for the new CEO as "great to work with," "creative," "clear vision," "perfect guy for the job."

As for Kallet, his goal was to grow Oneida Ltd. via acquisitions and new products.[14]

The FY 1999 annual report acknowledged some "growing pains" and some assorted problems which included restructuring reductions, new product-launch delays in dinnerware and glass, dealer inventory reductions, Asian turmoil, and import competition. Yet, the company had just purchased Australian outfits called Stanley Rogers & Son and Westminster China for $5 million. Three new company-owned stores were opened in the U. K. and the company had a crack at the Chinese market and the German market as well. A new 206,000 square-foot warehouse distribution center was to be in operation by early 2000 near the Sherrill factory which, in turn, was not ignored as new forging and knife-welding equipment had been put in place there.

Although net sales were up by some 5.2%, net income had sunk to $19,750,000 in FY 1999 or down 32.2% from the previous year. Under the heading "Forward Looking Information" in the annual report, readers were cautioned that "changes in certain factors...could cause the company's future consolidated results to differ materially from these expressed herein." Among other things, the company had taken on an additional $20,000,000 in long-term debt during the year and inventories were up by $57,000,000 or over 40%. The annual report discreetly (and as it turned out, portentously) announced that "a separate mass market line, Oneida glassware, was launched at the end of 1998 to an excellent reception. Strong growth [$40 million in sales over the next three to five years according to Matthews] is expected from this line." A strong reaction would soon be forthcoming. Nonetheless, in honor of its 250th consecutive dividend, an extra dividend of 10 cents a share was declared and management believed the company had sufficient liquidity and lines of credit to fund future operations.[15]

Matthews officially signed off the following year, giving up his chairmanship to Kallet at the end of May 2000. In the annual report, shareholders were invited to share management's "enthusiasm and anticipation for the FY2000 financial rewards ahead." This was followed by the expressed hope that readers "will share our confidence and enthusiasm that we [the company] now have the resources in place to enhance shareholder value on a sustainable basis."[16] During the calendar year 2000, shareholder value had largely been bolstered by the closing of the Canadian factory, management realignment, employment reduction, product line elimination, and a 20% inventory reduction—a seeming reduction in corporate resources of various kinds other than management's "confidence and enthusiasm."

Among the product resources in place, was the two-year old (and soon to be killed) consumer dinnerware line on display in department stores and mass merchandisers. Traditional holloware offerings had been supplemented by new giftware items. Company stores continued to show their value in terms of sales, "inventory management and product cost containment." However, the commercial glassware venture had turned up a significant problem in 1999.

With the advent of Oneida's commercial line, Libbey Inc. of Toledo, Ohio, the main domestic supplier of commercial glassware, decided to do two things. First, Libbey would sue Oneida Ltd. for pattern infringement. Second, Libbey would make an unsolicited offer of $26.56 a share to Oneida's stockholders. Apparently Gary Moreau, at the time he was Oneida's president, had met with Libbey's president and informally discussed a merger.

Libbey perceived some commonality with Oneida. Like Oneida, it was heavily into foodservice dinnerware, having purchased Syracuse China in 1995. Further, Libbey had expanded into flatware with the purchase of World Tableware, an importer of stainless and formerly the hotel and restaurant division of International Silver—Oneida's ancient and now defunct rival. Following Moreau's departure, Libbey had made several attempts to discuss such a takeover or merger with Oneida management and had been rebuffed on each occasion. Moreau was now on Libbey's board. While he claimed to have provided Libbey with no inside Oneida information, he let it be known he was strongly in favor of the proposed strategic buy-out of Oneida Ltd. by Libbey.

In April 1999, Libbey improved its offer to $30 a share and in July to $37.50. This offer was rejected by Oneida's board. Certain large investors must have blinked as they watched Oneida's share price rise significantly from its mid-$20s price prior to the Libbey offer. Now they would have to await share appreciation the slow way as Oneida went forward to improve its corporate profit performance.

In turning down Libbey's offer, Oneida management cited a lack of committed Libbey financing, possible anti-trust problems, Libbey's law suit to prevent Oneida's entrance into commercial glass, Oneida's newly implemented strategic plan intended to save $20 million in costs a year, and, finally, company earnings that had increased 25% in the first quarter of the current year. The proposed repurchase of 825,000 shares of company stock was also announced.

A special tent meeting of shareholders was held May 31st on the north lawn of the Mansion House at which Matthews, Chairman of the Board, made his last public appearance in an official corporate capacity. He told the large audience how he had acquired 1.4% of Oneida Ltd.'s common stock and had thus become its largest private stock holder. He then went on to say that if $37.50 a share was not good enough for him, why should it be good enough for anyone else? The loyal stockholders attending agreed with him, though those who did not sell once the Libbey offer had been withdrawn lived to regret it.

The Syracuse paper reported that, when Libbey withdrew its offer, that company's president said, "Oneida's entrenched management is intent on remaining a stand-alone company regardless of implications for its shareholders and employees." Oneida's stock was now at $27.85. The defense against the takeover attempt and Libbey lawsuit would cost Oneida $18,300,000 in legal expenses and, in a few short years, the company would withdraw from the sale of commercial glassware (which had provoked Libbey) and other new ventures of the 1990s.[17]

Following this drama, year-end results for fiscal year 2000 seemed almost anticlimactic. After an increase of $57,000,000 the year before, inventory had been reduced by $6,600,000. $41,300,000 in "restructuring costs" were logged including $11,000,000 to close the Canadian plant and, as mentioned, $18,300,000 to get Libbey off the corporate back. Net income staggered in at $5,500,000, down $14,240,000 from the previous year. Long-term debt was up by about $9,000,000 for the year, but still under control with stockholder equity exceeding long-term debt by 35%.[18]

Although he remained as board chairman through May 2000, Matthews had officially retired in December. Perhaps his greatest legacy to the company was the change in atmospherics he brought about. A practical thinker, his personal qualities of openness, ability to communicate, amiability, and objectivity attracted support within the organization to compensate for his lack of training or experience in any of the company's major functions. He ruled with a light touch believing that he should let his managers manage. The corollary of this is that such managers have to know how to manage, which was not always the case.

A strong trademark, well-advertised and well-positioned products combined with the good marketing conditions of the late 1980s and 1990s, and periodic cost reduction efforts led to good but variable net-income dollar results over Matthews' years as president. Fiscal year 1998 was the best year ever for Oneida Ltd. in terms of net income even after deducting a non-operational gain of $2,600,000. Matthews' last year, FY2000, would see net profit decline by almost 80% from this peak.[19]

A couple of financial disappointments during the 1990s which contributed to the ongoing "red" (that is, product being manufactured above standard cost) were factory variances at Buffalo China and a product-costing error at the Mexican factory which had to be expensively written down over several years. To this could be added the decline in profitability of the once lucrative Camden Wire company.

Company shareholders enjoyed a number of stock splits during Matthews' tenancy and also saw long-term debt increase by nearly 100%. However, the relationship between long-term debt and stockholder's equity remained about the same as it had been in 1987. Great violence was imminent in this area. Capital spending was substantial from 1987 to 1999 and much was spent on Buffalo China. Importantly, the nation experienced its greatest sustained economic expansion of the 20th century during these years which, combined with a weakened dollar from the strong and destructive dollar of the 1980s and a stronger yen, were of substantial competitive help to all domestic manufacturers.

Of the company's major initiatives, the record is somewhat spotty. The substantial expansion of the factory stores generated sales revenue and factory volume that was very helpful in regulating production and inventories. Almost all the stores, however, were later closed. Impact on the company's independent retailers is unknown. Two attempts at company-owned, high-end retail outlets were expensive failures. The purchase of a wholesaler was a doubtful undertaking which did not generate the benefits foreseen. New product launches such as palladium plate and New Domain stainless flatware and Acrylic "glassware" were unsuccessful. However, the importation of high quality German glassware did well.

Product quality was reduced by the elimination of both water-ground knife blades on medium-grade stainless and grade-rolling on Community-grade forks by way of lowering manufacturing cost—a futile gesture of trying to fight imports by reducing quality. Stainless flatware backstamps, regardless of quality grades, were altered to say: "Oneida USA." No longer were such familiar names as "Heirloom," "Community," and "Oneidacraft Deluxe" to be employed on the product to distinguish quality and cost. Consumers could now buy the Oneida name on the cheap. It was as if General Motors eliminated such marks as "Cadillac," "Buick," etc., in order to have all its cars called "General Motors USA." Additionally, imported product with the Oneida name on it was routinely available in discounters such as Wal-Mart. The Special Sales Division, always relied on to supply factory-unit volume, had substantially fallen off its flatware sales.

Matthews was definitely the best paid president to preside over Oneida Ltd. His total cash salary including cash incentives came to about $4,600,000 for the period FY1988-1998.[20] On top of this, he received restricted stock awards, stock options and "other compensation" which included allocated shares and matching payments to his 401K account—a true bonanza by traditional Oneida Ltd. standards. Matthews could look forward to a comfortable retirement as the Supplemental Retirement Plan (SERP) instituted by his predecessor would provide him with close to 50% of his average annual income less any "other retirement benefits."

Optimism for 1998
This annual report's theme, "Your Table is Ready," captures the thrust of our strategy to be a complete and fully balanced tableware company. In the last two years we have taken many steps to make that strategy a success, and we will continue in that direction in 1998. The tableware business has always been what we have done best, and our recent financial results certainly reflect that. We are optimistic about this year, thanks to the ongoing performance of our established business lines, as well as the aggressive new initiatives we are taking. We have a dedicated employee force, and we look forward to 1998 with anticipation.

WILLIAM D. MATTHEWS
Chairman of the Board and Chief Executive Officer

PETER J. KALLET
President and Chief Operating Officer

Along with the appointment of Kallet as his successor, a part of Matthew's legacy must also include the appointment, during his term in office, of eight members of the eleven-person board of directors. These board members would approve, in fiscal 2001, the fateful purchase of three companies thus lumbering Oneida Ltd. with a load of long-term debt which it could not repay, debt that was over twice the value of stockholder's equity; debt composed 40% of "good will;" debt that had to be largely repaid in three years; debt that, exclusive of fiscal year 1993, exceeded the total of the company's net earnings over the past ten years.

The proxy statement for Matthew's last year would list Allan H. Conseur for the first time as Executive Vice President at a salary in excess of President Pete Kallet's. In fact, only two people listed among the top incomes in the previous year were among the five shown in the proxy statement of 2000.[21] Things were about to take a violent turn for the worse.

At the moment Matthews retired, a major plan to restructure was announced. To reduce overhead expense and improve cash flow, 130 early retirements would take place and 50 "overhead" positions would be eliminated.

Notes to Chapter 6

1 Vice President Tom Ross quoted in *Oneida Daily Dispatch*, July 29, 1986.
2 Oneida Ltd. Annual Report for Fiscal Year Ended January 31, 1987; Oneida Ltd. press release, "Oneida Ltd. Reports 3rd Quarter Results," November 25, 1986.
3 Oneida Ltd. Annual Report for Fiscal Years Ended January 31, 1987, 13, and January 30, 1988, 2.
4 Oneida Ltd. Annual Report for Fiscal Year Ended January 27, 1990.
5 David N. Waller, "Corporate leader has local ties," *Rome Daily Sentinel*, September 21, 1989.
6 Oneida Ltd. Annual Report for Fiscal Years Ended January 26, 1991, 1, and January 25, 1997, 1; Kenneth L. Fisher, "Damn lies," *Forbes*, December 21, 1992, 339.
7 Oneida Ltd. Annual Report for Fiscal Year Ending January 28, 1995, inside front cover.
8 Elizabeth Doran, "Youthful Boss Sets Sterling Example," *Syracuse Post-Standard*, May 9, 1992.
9 Oneida Ltd. Annual Report for Fiscal Year Ended January 25, 1997, 16.
10 Oneida Ltd. Annual Report for Fiscal Year Ended January 25, 1997, 18.
11 Oneida Ltd. Annual Report for Fiscal Year Ended January 25, 1997, 3.

12 Oneida Ltd. Annual Report for Fiscal Years Ended January 25, 1997 ("strategic moves" quoted from inside front cover) and January 31, 1998, 2.
13 Oneida Ltd. Annual Report for Fiscal Year Ending January 31, 1998, 2, and Oneida Ltd. Proxy Statement, April 24, 1998, 7.
14 Oneida Ltd. Annual Report for Fiscal Year Ending January 30, 1999, inside front cover; Linda Murphy, "Growth: A personal, professional goal for Kallet," *Syracuse Observer-Dispatch*, November 1, 1998.
15 Oneida Ltd. Annual Report for Fiscal Year Ending January 30, 1999, 2, 8, 30.
16 Oneida Ltd. Annual Report for Fiscal Year Ended January 29, 2000, 2-3.
17 Charley Hannagan, "Oneida Ltd. fights takeover," *Syracuse Post-Standard*, April 29, 1999; Oneida Ltd. press release, "Oneida Board of Directors Rejects Libbey's Unsolicited Proposal: Board Authorizes Share Buyback," July 6, 1999; James T. Mulder, "Libbey drops Oneida takeover," *Syracuse Observer-Dispatch*, July 16, 1999.
18 Oneida Ltd. Annual Report for Fiscal Year Ended January 29, 2000, 13, 28.
19 Oneida Ltd. Annual Report for Fiscal Years Ended January 31, 1998, 13, and January 29, 2000, 13.
20 Computed from Oneida Ltd. Proxy Statements such as those of April 24, 1998, 7, and April 23, 1999, 7, which provide figures for 1995-1998.
21 "Oneida launches restructuring to reduce costs, improve operations," *The Oneida Silversmith*, Winter 1999, 1; Oneida Ltd. Proxy Statement, April 24, 2000, 7.

7

Peter J. Kallet, 1999-2006

When Bill Matthews introduced Pete Kallet to the Oneida management group as the future CEO, he stressed "integrity" as the key virtue of leadership. Having been chosen by Matthews to be, first, Oneida Ltd.'s president and then eventual CEO as a result of Gary Moreau's abrupt departure, Kallet brought to the job a varied company background and apparent success as head of the foodservice division. After attending Utica College, he joined Oneida's accounting department, then moved swiftly into consumer sales. In this latter capacity, he covered upstate New York and, subsequently, an Ohio territory following which he returned to the home office in product and purchasing management. His next move was into foodservice sales management and, when the two executives ahead of him retired, Pete became divisional head of sales. His was a low-key personality, affable and reassuring. He seemed personable and articulate and, since he apparently had a good sales record, he was generally (with some reservations) well received in his new position.

Serving under Matthews for five years, Kallet had the opportunity to become familiar with the scope of the CEO's job, to work on his own ideas, and to develop his relationship with the firm and its employees. Matthews said he had no reservations concerning Kallet as his successor and that Pete was the right man to succeed him. Kallet, for his part, said his "style was never to campaign to get the next job."[1]

Business was good during those years with net sales rising by 36% from fiscal year 1993 (last year to include Camden Wire sales) to Matthews' last year, fiscal year 2000. The economy was booming, the stock market was in heat and Oneida's net income, always struggling historically to achieve 4% on net sales, was not only 4% for each of these years, but also hit 5.9% in fiscal 1998. But there is a business cliché that warns: "The decisions that kill you are the ones made when times are good." This would come true with a vengeance for Oneida Ltd. in a few short years. However, when Matthews retired, the company was in sound fiscal shape and its immediate prospects looked promising.

The sale of Camden had paid for the purchase of Rego China in 1996 which filled an upscale market niche from Buffalo China's products. The balance sheet for fiscal 2000 was in good shape with current assets exceeding current liabilities by $145 million or 49%. The "acid test" ratio (cash and cash equivalent only) was another matter inasmuch as only 64% of current liabilities were covered by current assets. Long-term debt was 74% of stockholder's equity. The operating statement was not looking good as net income had fallen to 1.1% of net sales.

> **Stockholders' Equity to Total Liabilities.** The exact proportion of owners' capital and borrowed capital is provided by this ratio. Under normal conditions one would expect a ratio of 150 to 200 per cent in a furniture manufacturing business.
>
> | Stockholders' equity ($000) | 625 | 595 | 622 |
> |---|---|---|---|
> | Total liabilities ($000) | 688 | 657 | 689 |
> | Ratio or percentage (%) | 90.84 | 90.56 | 90.29 |
>
> The creditors actually control the business, and exercise of their control can be expected momentarily.
>
> **Stockholders' Equity to Fixed Assets.** Do the stockholders own the plant and equipment? This would appear to be the minimum investment expected of owners.

Illustration of Stockholders Equity

Some ominous developments occurring in calendar year 1999 were to gather strength—if that's the word—over the next few years. Restructuring costs, a plant closing in Canada, long-term asset impairments, and other "unusual charges" (i.e., Libbey fallout) cost about $44 million.[2] For work of this sort, Kallet received an annual salary compensation of $696,000 exclusive of long-term compensation but including cash incentive of $337,620—a one-year record for Oneida. One can only imagine what he might have received for a good year. After announcing some plant closings and intended job eliminations that year, Kallet concluded that company prospects could scarcely be better: "With our state of the manufacturing and logistic capabilities, we strongly believe that we have laid the basis for success and the creation of shareholder value for years to come."[3]

Fiscal year 2000 net sales were up by 6.3% with dinnerware up 14.9% (Rego effect), and the new commercial glass line sales increased by 90% to $37,000,000. However, metal products, of which stainless flatware was by far the most important and which had paid the freight since the late 1950s, had flat sales of $337,600,000. At $5,500,000, net profits were down by over $14,000,000 from the previous year.

There was a certain symmetry to the Millennial Year 2000. The Oneida Community had attempted in 1848 to introduce a new millennium—"Perfectionism," a new relationship among humans which eventually failed in its social theory but succeeded in its economic enterprises. The millennial year of 2000 would see the Community's successor, Oneida Ltd., lay the seeds that would lead to both corporate economic collapse and reneging on the company's traditional concern for its employees' economic and social welfare. But, let's begin when the debacle began.

The president's letter in the annual report for fiscal 2001 talked of "the growth strategy embraced in the mid-1990s"—*everything for the tabletop for both consumers and restaurants*. It soon proved to be a doomed strategy as good quality, lower priced flatware imports flooded in on Oneida's single-product dependence. A "seasoned management team" was in place to attend to strategy and administration and "the largest sales force in the industry" would see that customers received the benefits of owning the company's greatly increased range of tabletop products.[4]

With regard to the product range, Oneida purchased, for cash and in rapid succession, a series of companies in the tabletop business. On June 13, 2000, Viners of Sheffield, Ltd. was had for $25,000,000 cash.[5] Viners, an established competitor of the company's English affiliate, had long given up manufacturing, gone broke a couple of times, and had, for years, been an importer of Far Eastern tableware products and, latterly, a retailer of same through a few company operated outlets.

Next to be acquired was Sakura, Inc., based in New York City, an importer and marketer of imported dinnerware. Two weeks after the Viners deal, Sakura was purchased on June 30th at a cost of $40,000,000 in cash.[6]

In August, Oneida Ltd. bought Delco for approximately $60,000,000 in cash. This outfit was based on Long Island and imported tableware products for the foodservice trade. It later turned out that a further $18,000,000 had been set aside to integrate Delco with Oneida and to make additional payments to its previous owners.[7]

In order to pull all this off, Oneida had to borrow $275,000,000 on a three-year revolving credit basis. Some of this borrowed money was being used to "refinance the majority of the company's outstanding credit facilities." At this point (June 2, 2000), long-term debt became twice the value of stockholder's equity: about $238 million versus $124 million. Why would banks permit such financial imbalance? Perhaps it was the prospect of handsome interest to be paid by a company with a past record of financial conservatism and prompt payment.

No explanation was ever given for the seemingly extravagant prices paid for these companies and why Oneida stock was not used in conjunction with cash. One possibility is that stock was ruled out due to concern over share dilution and the consequent need for shareholder approval. As for the prices paid, the only seeming justification would have been the current strength of the acquisitions' earnings, cash flow, and future prospects for the growth of same. However, these acquisitions had no apparent tangible assets other than inventories and accounts receivable. As it was, the total immediate bills for buying these companies came to $125,000,000 of which goodwill represented $114,732,000 or over 92% of the combined purchase price. All of this occurred in a time of $39,000,000 worth of restructuring cost, consequent job loss and closing of the storied Canadian factory.[8]

Relevant audited financial statements of the acquired companies would include, at a bare minimum, several consecutive years of balance sheets, operating statements, cash flow reports, and fiscal projections. This information would give a good idea of the sales and profit history and the plans and prospects for the acquired companies and why, in consequence, Oneida wanted to buy them at the prices that were paid. Such records were never made available (as of June 2012) for independent review. Based on the available evidence, the purchase of these companies—Viners, Sakura, and Delco—was probably not justified by their past performances and future prospects at the time of purchase.

When asked about board discussions leading up to the purchase of the three companies and whether financial data justified purchase, Kallet said that "fiduciary responsibility" prevented him from discussing these matters. A "fiduciary relationship" in business is generally understood to be a position of trust, meaning that a corporate director is trusted by the shareholders to manage their investment and trusted, as well, by the employees with what amounts to their security.

There is limited information on the most expensive of these importers of tableware product that can be extracted from Form 8K/A (dated October 28, 2000), headed (roughly) "Oneida Ltd....and Delco...Unaudited pro forma balance sheets as of July 29, 2000." Delco, a purveyor of cheap, low quality stainless flatware largely to the catering business, produced the following unaudited figures for the half year just prior to its purchase by Oneida. (A single half-year's result provides no idea of trends.)

Delco Income Statement
Unaudited

	Half Year- 29 July 2000 (000s)	Full Year- 31 Jan. 2000 (000s)
Net Sales	$38,308	$75,662
Cost of Sales	$26,801 (70%)	$52,132 (69%)
Gross Profit	$11,507 (30%)	$23,530 (31%)
Sales & GA	$10,277 (26.8%)	$14,790 (19.5%)
Operating Income	$1,230 (3.2%)	$8,240 (11.5%)
Profit before Tax	$714 (1.9%)	$8.018 (10.5%)
Tax	$297	$3,282
Net Profit	$417 (1.1%)	$4,736 (6.2%)

Oneida borrowed $61,000,000 to buy Delco. A non-compete agreement was to add $8,650,000 to this cost and, ultimately, the purchase price would look more like $76,000,000.

Delco Balance Sheet
Unaudited

	Half Year- 29 July 2000 (000s)	Full Year- 31 Jan. 2000 (000s)
Assets	$34,789	$33,473
Liabilities	$17,304	$11,081
Stockholders' Equity	$17,485	$17,067

With net assets of $17 million and a purchase price of $76 million, goodwill came close to $60 million. Oneida Ltd. had borrowed $61 million for this acquisition at rates ranging from 8.5% to 10.75%. Using 10%, the annual interest cost would be $6.1 million blotting up over 75% of the pre-tax profit of $8 million. In the best case, after paying interest expense, it would be many years before Delco would pay off the debt incurred for its purchase. Delco must have been expected to grow substantially in sales and profits. Perhaps cost-saving synergies were anticipated? Since Delco's results were amalgamated with Oneida's after purchase, there is no public record of how this purchase might have begun to pay back.

The 2001 annual report also provided a pro-forma of the operations of the acquired companies as if the acquisitions had occurred on January 31, 1999. For fiscal years 2001 and 2000, the three acquisitions on this basis would have added $55.1 million and $116 million in net sales respectively. The full year pro-forma indicates Oneida would have had a loss of $4,462,000 in fiscal year 2001 versus an actual loss of $1,300,000 and a profit in fiscal year 2000 of $3,868,000 compared to an actual profit of $5,500,000. The apparent increase in net loss and reduction in net income despite increased sales could be attributed to increased interest expense. However, the pro-forma does not spell this out.

A new line in the 2001 annual report, showing up under "Accrued Liabilities," indicated "accrued acquisition costs" of $7,579,000. Other increases in accruals featured an increase in employee benefits of $3.8 million and interest payable of $1.9 million. Also, interest expense doubled from the previous year to $21,602,000. A note payable of $246,500,000 had been added at interest rates varying from 6.5% to 10.75% with loan payment of total long-term debt rising by $184,320,000 overall from fiscal year 2000. $253,414,000 was due in fiscal 2004, three years hence. This would be the last time financial results for the three acquisitions would appear in the annual report due to their amalgamation within the overall results shown for international operations, dinnerware, and metal flatware.

In the meantime, the company was cutting costs by way of scaling back production and eliminating jobs. Although $24 million of inventory write-down represented product rationalization resulting from recent acquisitions, total inventory went up by $32 million. Overall, the company lost $1,300,000 in the fiscal year 2001.[9]

Most individual total incomes were down from the previous year due to an understandable decrease in cash-incentive pay. Management, however, apparently paid themselves more. Base salaries for five executives improved by a total of $192,000. Further, and while the company was losing money, the same individuals were enriched by $531,000 in total cash incentives.[10]

Another ominous note was sounded in a September phone call I received from the head of a market research company once employed by Oneida. That individual reported that, 2.5 years before, Oneida's patterns had 50% of all "upstairs" sales in department stores but that had now fallen to 30%. As of the year 2000, the sale of Oneida's older patterns had slowed down, the company's newer patterns were not going well, and, overall, six out of the twelve best-selling patterns were Oneida's—not ten of twelve as had been the case three years before.

The company continued, during early 2001, to reduce inventory and employees while Oneida dividends had been cut in half. Overall gross profit was down by 9% from the previous year although sales were up by 7%, perhaps demonstrating the effect of the recent acquisitions. Interest expenses increased by 144% to $7.1 million from the first quarter of fiscal 2000, effectively wiping out operating income and leaving the company with earnings of two cents a share on April 28, 2001, versus forty-five cents the year before.

The ensuing months featured more of the same. By the beginning of May 2001, 575 jobs had been eliminated, 330 from the Sherrill plant. At the end of the second quarter, gross profit had improved substantially over the previous year-to-date, and despite increased selling and administrative expenses, operating profit came to about $16 million. With $13 million of interest expenses, net income of only $2.1 million was left. Total long-term debt was down by $2.7 million and earnings per share for six months came to 13 cents. According to a news report of May 1, 2001, the company was forecasting earnings per share for the full year at 85 cents and sales to hit $580 million. "Oneida," the article explained, "had chosen to battle the slumping economy by cutting jobs, products, inventory and debt." Also mentioned were some manufacturing changes. Six patterns made overseas were to be made in Sherrill, while twenty-four home-made patterns would be produced overseas.[11] Business was down some and debt was well up as the company approached September 11, 2001, and the terrorist attacks in New York City and Washington, D. C.

According to a company memorandum in late September, total order income after 9/11 was down by 30-35% with retail off 25% and foodservice sales off 50% with annual sales to airlines of about $25 million probably gone forever. Only international sales were on target.[12]

A month later, the company newsletter indicated consumer sales were encouraging but that foodservice was still in a slump as people were not traveling. Home Store sales were recovering at a faster pace than the other divisions and reduced travel was not impacting international sales. Kallet was asked: "Did Oneida overextend with the major acquisitions in 2000?" "Absolutely not," he replied. The acquisitions not only contributed significantly to Oneida profits, they provided valuable new management talent as well as market growth. The lost airline business, he added, would reduce sales by $12-15 million the following year.[13]

The *Oneida Daily Dispatch* (October 30, 2001) related that very low earnings per share could be expected from third quarter results, that inventory had been cut further, that debt was down by $26 million compared to the previous year, and that factory work hours had been reduced. "These cost reduction measures," Kallet explained, "are key elements in helping us execute our previously announced strategic initiatives to lower our inventory and improve our cash flow in order to further reduce our debt." Thus, debt had readjusted the strategic sights from producing everything for the table top to the immediate need to produce cash to pay down debt. However, Kallet reassured the reader, Oneida was strengthening its foundation for the long term and providing maximum value to its shareholders.

Shortly after, a company press release (November 14, 2001) gave the following financial results for the first nine months of the year. Despite the weakened economy and terrorist attack, overall net sales were the same as they were the previous year (for the same period) with gross profit up by $10.7 million and operating income by $16.7 million. Interest expense rose by $4.8 million and, through nine months, core earnings came in at 14 cents a share versus $1.18 for the same period the year before. Long-term debt was down $10.6 million to $272.2 million.

When published in late April of 2002, the annual report for the full year attempted to put a brave face on what increasingly looked like impending disaster. The president's letter spoke heroically about "making the right choices for the long term good of the company," and meted out praise for the "skills and productivity of our workforce" (an ever-diminishing body whose selfless character was saluted). Long-term debt had been paid down by over $26 million and inventories were reduced by over $45 million. With it all, long-term debt was now twice the total of stockholder's equity and working capital was down by $16 million at year end. This result was brought about largely by the absence of "restructuring and unusual charges" which had cost $15,008,000 the previous year. Yet, despite the recession and 9/11 after-effect, net sales were only a little over 3% behind the previous year, gross profit was up by about 1%, operating income by around 50%, and net income of 1.7% was reported. Not a robust performance but an improvement over the fiscal year 2001's net loss of $1.3 million.

Accrued acquisition costs of $7,579,000 had popped up in the notes accompanying the previous year's annual report. Such costs were down to $3,436,000 in fiscal year 2002. However, the report on long-term debt was that the company and its lenders negotiated revised covenant levels. In fact, the parties had entered into a security agreement which collateralized the company's debt "with all of the domestic assets (excluding real estate holdings)."

At the end of the fourth quarter of 2002, the company was still not in compliance with its interest agreements. It entered into a Waiver and Amendment with its lenders leading to an extension of maturity of revolving debt and also to include Oneida's domestic real estate holdings among collateral pledged. Limitations were also placed on "dividends, capital expenditures, inter-company indebtedness and letter of credit."

All this fancy language meant that Oneida Ltd. was in hock up to its eyeballs.[14] As things stood on January 26, 2001, the company had to figure out how to meet long-term debt maturity of about $231 million in fiscal year 2004 out of total long-term debt of $260 million. For the current and past five fiscal years, cumulative income from continuing operations had come to $116.5 million.

"Excess purchase price over net fair value," i.e., goodwill, was beginning to be written down over a 40-year period but still totaled over $134 million. The most flagrant "excess purchase price" was paid to the owners of Delco International. The annual report said that "following significant foodservice sales decline after 9/11," the company expected to regain all its foodservice business, with the possible exception of flatware sales to airlines, *which are not material* [emphasis added]. That seemed ironic in view of the fact that Delco was a prime supplier of cheap flatware to the airlines and catering trade. Shareholders were reassured, however, that the company was "emphasizing professional experience and educational background in top management positions"—a statement that might have been difficult to substantiate with the facts on hand.[15]

As the company celebrated 125 years of flatware manufacturing in 2002, it announced an innovative concept called "lean manufacturing." This was a policy designed to reduce cost of production and to make short production runs profitable, and thus provide rapid response to customer needs while tightening inventory control. These improvements would provide competitive advantage over imported products. "Lean manufacturing" was to be fully functional by the end of calendar year 2004.[16]

Annual reports had consistently stressed Oneida's 90% name recognition among customers. Oneida's consumer franchises had been the best thing to talk about in recent times and, in fact, the annual report for fiscal 2003 featured a review of the company's advertising. Early 20th-century emphasis had been on individual brands: Community Plate and later various Rogers trademarks with occasional ads for Heirloom Sterling and, later, Oneida. It was in 1960 that the company decided upon promoting "Corporate Recognition," that is, the Oneida name rather than individual brands. With excellent illustration and copy approach (e.g., "Look again, It's Stainless"), innovative design (e.g., the Chateau pattern), improved manufacturing capability, thorough-going market distribution, and—of course—excellent quality, with all of that the company forged ahead of its competition. And, as explained in Chapter 3, an extensive consumer sampling program via national advertising put millions of stainless teaspoons in American homes where advertising claims for the product could be judged first-hand.

Furthermore, the company had always been fussy about the publications it used and the page position in which its advertisements appeared. Even when economic conditions were challenging, the company had always believed in advertising continuity as each year presented a new set of consumers, in particular, brides. Advertising had been a sacred expenditure since the time of P. B. Noyes and the emergence of Community Plate in 1903.

But now, as Oneida's fortunes wound down and the need to generate cash went up, the advertising budget was reduced. The budget of $4,145,000 in fiscal 2001 was down to $2,643,000 by 2003. Fiscal year 2003's annual report mentioned that "the company has entered into various barter transactions exchanging inventory for barter credits to be utilized in the future on advertising, freight and other goods and services."[17] This did not sound much like effective advertising.

Financial results for fiscal year 2003 showed improvement over the previous year. Although net sales were down 4%, net income at $9.2 million was up over $2 million from revised fiscal 2002 results. Earnings per share improved to 55 cents from 42 cents, the latter figure having been restated from the 51 cents originally reported in the 2002 report. Sale of marketable securities totaled $8.4 million in FY 2003 and was about half the decrease in total net cash flow after cash flow from Operating Activities which declined by $17 million from the previous year.[18] The company had restated earnings for fiscal 2001 and 2002 and half of 2003. This had the unfortunate effect of putting the company in arrears regarding its loan covenants.

On December 11, 2002, the Board of Directors awarded four company managers, including Kallet, handsome retirement packages to be paid for by life annuities. This was followed up with a similar arrangement for the short-timer, Allan Conseur, on April 8, 2004. On May 1, the company took a $540,000 charge from New York State for "amending its pension plan to add executive obligations." The Annual Report for fiscal year 2004 stated, "since Oct. 25th, 2003, the company has been in violation of the interest coverage ratio, leverage ratio and net worth covenants and received a series of waivers from its lenders to expire June 15, 2004."

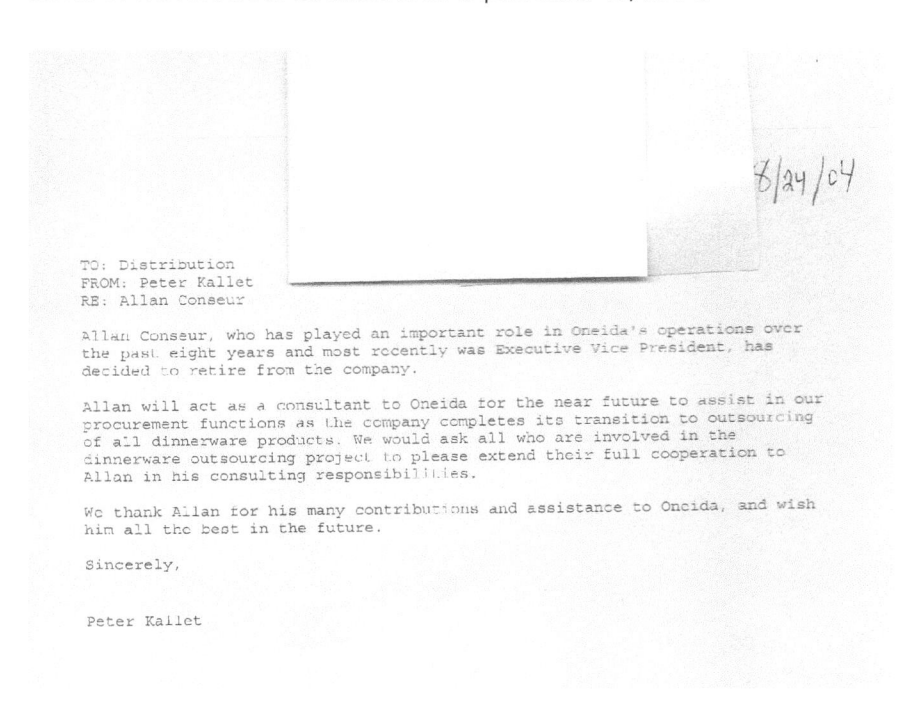

8/24/04

TO: Distribution
FROM: Peter Kallet
RE: Allan Conseur

Allan Conseur, who has played an important role in Oneida's operations over the past eight years and most recently was Executive Vice President, has decided to retire from the company.

Allan will act as a consultant to Oneida for the near future to assist in our procurement functions as the company completes its transition to outsourcing of all dinnerware products. We would ask all who are involved in the dinnerware outsourcing project to please extend their full cooperation to Allan in his consulting responsibilities.

We thank Allan for his many contributions and assistance to Oneida, and wish him all the best in the future.

Sincerely,

Peter Kallet

Thus, as the financial clouds began to gather, the company extracted what would eventually come to over $12,500,000 (estimated) from its under-funded pension plan assets in order to provide a "a special benefit" for the five people involved. The leading beneficiary was Kallet at $301,163 a year, followed by $246,000 for Conseur (up from $33,000), followed by lesser amounts of around $100,000 plus or minus for three others.[19] Between 2002 and 2004, the *Wall Street Journal* (January 18, 2004) remarked, the pension plan's funding dropped from a feeble 55% to 43% of commitment.

2004 featured further news about Oneida's pension plan. A week after providing Conseur's "special benefit," the company failed "to make a quarterly funding contribution of $939,951 to the employee pension plan." Two weeks later, on May 1st, Oneida took the previously mentioned "$540,000 first quarter charge for amending its pension plan to add the executive obligations." The company held out until June 7th to freeze the pension plan "closing it to new participants and halting the buildup of additional benefits for participants." The freeze did not affect the special executive benefits because they were already set at a "fixed amount." Finally, pension fund activity for year 2004 concluded July 15 with Oneida filing "to make mandatory quarterly funding contributions of $1.3 million to the pension plan." (All remarks in quotation above are from the *Wall Street Journal*'s online View-all-and-Print, January 18, 2010.)

So, the company drew at least $12,500,000 from the pension fund to provide annuitized special retirement benefits for five people. At the same time, it was not making two mandatory funding contributions totaling $2,239,951 to the fund and was being fined $540,000 for raiding the fund.

Cash flow had now become critical to the company's hope to stave off bankruptcy. In fiscal 2004, between long-term debt maturities and non-cancelable operating leases, the company would have to lay out $221 million by the end of fiscal year 2005. Where was this money to come from? The fiscal year 2003 had seen negative cash flow of $8.5 million. In his president's letter, Pete Kallet felt "sustained by the basic appeal of the Oneida name" and reported that sales for the final quarter had increased—the first such increase since 9/11.[20]

The highest paid individual listed in the proxy statement took a 4% salary reduction, perhaps in line with the 4% reduction in net sales the company had experienced. However, clouded the company's prospects might be, however, those people could look forward to a happy financial future. Recall that in the 1980s, the company had set up a Supplemental Executive Retirement Plan (SERP) which rewarded key employees with 40 to 50% of their annual salary upon retirement. In 2003, the company adopted an unfunded benefit restoration plan for certain employees designed as similar to the SERP which provided the previously mentioned "special benefits."[21]

Various mutual funds now owned 70% of the company's stock, but those still invested in early 2004 must have been becoming anxious. The Utica newspaper reported in late 2002 that Ariel Capital Management, now Oneida's largest shareholder, considered this stock "a good long-term investment." Mr. Morton, an enthusiastic senior Vice President of this mutual fund, was quoted as saying, "after decades of neglect, you [Oneida] now have a management team very cost conscious." He continued to exude such optimism into March. But Ariel sold its Oneida stake very shortly after and Mr. Morton would no longer be following Oneida fortunes.[22]

The spring of the year had seen a continuation of the slowness in consumer and foodservice orders, this situation being attributed to depressed consumer confidence and now the Iraq War. Net corporate loss for the first half of fiscal 2004 year came to $7.1 million and the factory was down to 1,100 employees from 2,500 workers five years before.

Hints had also been given that the company's last remaining factory in Sherrill would be closed if "lean manufacturing" did not produce $18 million in annual cost savings. The company was looking to save a total of $30 million a year from plant changes as well as lean manufactures. Asset stripping had begun with the sale of the employee golf course and the Lewis Point recreational area on Oneida Lake for about $3 million.

In December 2003, it was announced that lean manufacturing was about 70% installed in the Sherrill factory. Presumably, the remaining 30% could be up and running well ahead of the deadline set for December 2004. Kallet said the company was well positioned for recovery. On the subject of having its own factory ("better market control, speed of order response, made in USA"), Pete also said the "lean" would be evaluated in the first quarter of calendar year 2004 and that the Oneida name was not worth more than a 20% price premium despite its 90% recognition among consumers.[23] With what had happened in recent times to product quality, backstamp, retail exposure, and greatly reduced national advertising, this dim value judgment may have become true.

The third quarter of the fiscal year continued the dismal financial results with a loss of $74.8 million, $41 million of which could be attributed to plant closing costs. Waivers on loan repayments had become standard practice by this time and would continue until the company's eventual bankruptcy.

Business continued poorly into calendar year 2004 with Kallet telling *Forbes* magazine that "we [Oneida] had five years of sales growth [to 2001] and we did not pay attention to internal workings." He might as easily have pointed to too much attention paid to external workings and to an acquisition binge of destructive proportions. Layoffs and loan repayment waivers continued.

Now outside experts were being hired for $3.1 million to help the company restructure its credit "facilities." In March, the company was talking to an equity investor. In May, the company retained Carl Marks Consulting Group LLC which the *Syracuse Post Standard* described as experts on strategic advice, debt restructuring, and product sourcing (May 1, 2004). Also, Peter J. Solomon Co., counselors in strategic financial planning and mergers and acquisitions, had been retained. At this point, Oneida Ltd. had $243 million in long-term debt and had just received its eighth payment waiver.

The Oneida newspaper's editorial of April 3rd ("Many Paying Price for Company's Miscalculation") noted it was "clear that Oneida Ltd. made some bad moves in taking on a lot of debt." Stock was now at $1.20 a share. Amendments to employee benefit plans had been put in place and severance pay for dismissed employees was under consideration in April. A thirty-year employee could look forward to two weeks severance, something that would have made P. B. Noyes roll in his grave. Parenthetically, Libbey was also experiencing a slow economy, a war in Iraq, and a SARS epidemic in eastern Asia. Unlike Oneida, however, Libbey was surviving these challenges in good shape.[24] One wonders how Libbey would have done if they had bought Oneida for around $70 million?

It had been announced in April that Oneida Ltd.'s annual report would be delayed due to some technical reporting problem. In mid-May, the company's outside accountants, PricewaterhouseCoopers LLC, resigned and the New York Stock Exchange delisted Oneida's stock. The company reacted by cutting wages, freezing its pension plan, and eliminating health insurance for retirees. "It was a beautiful company for so many years," employees began to say.

Along with the outside accountants, the traditional annual report also was gone. The 2004 annual statement comprised a glossy cover embracing the company's 10-K report, a tangible demonstration of austerity compared to the handsome annual publications that had preceded it. The four-page cover contained Pete Kallet's presidential letter, some pretty pictures, and the last listing of corporate officers and directors to be named by an independent Oneida Ltd.

Kallet's remarks dealt with an assortment of asset sales, "a variable cost sourcing system instead of a fixed-cost factory system" (e.g., importing goods from East Asia, etc.) and some faint hopes for the future and "strengthening our shareholder value." He described the year ending in January 2004 as "one of major transition for your company," or perhaps better said, what was left of it. In fact, the company had transitioned from a net profit of $9.2 million in fiscal 2003 to a loss of $99 million in fiscal 2004. Kallet, however, reassured alarmed stockholders, that "we now are better positioned for consistent performance regardless of market conditions."

"Better positioning" apparently meant the closing of five factories. This began with the sale of the Buffalo China plant to former management for $5.5 million. It had cost $17.4 million to purchase Buffalo China and another $11 million had been put into a new dinnerware warehouse. Along the way, various amounts of capital had also been spent on dinnerware factory equipment and a bisc (unfinished and undecorated rough dish or plate) factory in Mexico. Even though this added up to a staggering amount of capital spending, Kallet now said he believed that "our actions will lead to strengthening our shareholder value."[25]

The sale of this once highly profitable company was indicative of what was happening to Oneida Ltd. Four other plants had been closed for $10 million from which the costs associated with such sales would be deducted. The factories liquidated in November included two in Mexico and one each in China and Italy at a cost of $46 million. These moves were said to save $12 million a year but the stock was down to $4.73. Dividends, in fact, had been cancelled in August breaking a sixty-seven year run of continuous dividend payments.

A summary of this debacle showed that net sales for the year were 8% below the preceding year and gross margins at 22.9% versus 31.6% the previous year: less sales at lower gross profit—a deadly combination. The net loss for the fiscal year was $99.2 million versus a profit of $9.2 million in fiscal 2003. Restructuring and impairments contributed about $28 million to the loss with interest expense kicking in another $16.7 million and revision of loss carry-forwards cost another $25.3 million in *income* tax! Long-term debt was hovering at $223.2 million. Retained earnings went from $68.4 million positive in FY 2003 to minus $32.9 million in FY 2004.

Kallet and company were, and had been for some time, at the mercy of those from whom they had borrowed and not repaid in timely fashion. A truly horrible fiscal swamp.

Finally, the dismal 10-K came to an end with a list of over twenty waivers relating to corporate borrowing, the majority involving THC

Systems, Inc. (the dinnerware company purchased in 1996 and once run by Oneida's executive vice president), and to "employment agreements with five (5) executive employees of the company" dated November 19, 1999, along with the same for another executive employee dated May 11, 2000. As company finances sank under the direction of this team, its individual members appeared to be in decent financial shape. According to the proxy statement, their salaries rose, presumably on the merit of work performed in FY 2004.[26]

The annual and final meeting of stockholders took place in the historic Big Hall of the Oneida Community's Mansion House on May 26th, 2004. Armed guards were on hand for the first time at such a gathering to keep an eye on the large and outraged crowd. The failing management and board of directors were asked:

- "Why hadn't Pete Kallet been fired four years ago?"
- "Why were executive salaries raised while those of office and factory workers were cut?"
- "Why had the short-term executive vice president received a pension increase when the pensions of the rank-and-file had been frozen?"

The author addressing the last Mansion House Oneida Ltd. annual meeting

The audience responded vociferously as these questions were raised but never satisfactorily answered. The management seemed to have little to say and less that was germane. One director did remark that Kallet, under enormous stress, was doing "an incredible job." Certainly no one in that audience disagreed that the job Kallet did was "incredible."

"Why," it was then asked, "had the board of directors approved acquisitions whose cash cost had plunged the company so heavily into debt that could not now be repaid?" Kallet begged the question by saying that the acquisitions had been looked at for several years and that they all became available in the same year. According to one director quoted in the press (W. D. Pidot, a partner in the company's New York law firm), the acquisitions, which had cost $125 million including $114 million of goodwill, were bought "for the benefit of the company." "We did look into it," said he.[27] One would like to know what they saw by way of audited financial reports that would justify their purchase. Later, Mr. Pidot's law firm would handle Oneida Ltd.'s bankruptcy.

"Lenders to Take Control" of Oneida Ltd. announced the *Syracuse Post Standard* on June 26th, 2004. The company's debt of $235 million was to be re-financed. The lenders would provide $30 million in working capital and, for another $30 million, would buy 62% of the total stock Oneida was authorized to issue or thirty million shares. This burst of liquidity would stave off bankruptcy—for a while. With the debt now reduced to $235 million, Oneida Ltd. took on a three-year loan for $125 million and a three-and-a-half year loan for $80 million. Interest rates on these latter loans would be substantial. The company's board was to be reorganized with six seats going to nominees of the lenders. Pete Kallet was to remain on the board along with three other current directors.

Meanwhile, Oneida Ltd. continued to renege on its previous employee benefit plans. A pension supplement for middle managers was terminated July 13th along with a long-term disability plan. No "special benefit" at a "fixed amount" for these folks! Employee contributions to the existing health plans were increased. Also terminated were the employee stock purchase plan and executive stock options. There was a certain sad irony in these two moves inasmuch as stock was virtually worthless and the company was soon to be bankrupt.[28]

Kallet indicated in the late summer of 2004 that he felt encouraged with the company's financial restructuring. Then, on September 9th, he announced the closing of the Sherrill factory. "Lean manufacturing"—70%

installed since being initiated the previous December—came up four-and-a-half months short of demonstrating whether it could deliver the remaining 30% and thus produce the forecast $18 million in annual product-cost savings. The only explanation given for the decision was that factory costs had remained high. The Oneida newspaper quoted Kallet as saying "that the company already imports more flatware than it has been producing"—a sure formula for driving up volume variances. Five hundred jobs would now be gone by early 2005 and, with them, a great manufacturing heritage and the heartbeat of the community. "At the end of the day," Kallet philosophized, "you have to protect the company and its shareholders." The plant, he added, would never reopen. On the positive side, Kallet professed great confidence in his new overseas sourcing network.[29]

Two newly refinanced loans came to $205 million and the collateral for these loans was "a first priority lien over substantially all of the company's and its domestic subsidiary's assets." One loan could hit an interest rate high of 17%. The company may have to obtain further covenant waivers, an article in the Oneida paper concluded.[30] Later in the month, the Syracuse paper would announce that Oneida Ltd. had received another lien, this one from the Federal Pension Benefit Guaranty Corp for missing a $2.3 million payment to its pension fund. Accrued pension liabilities now came to $35 million and New York State was piling on with a tax warrant for $895.00 against the company for overdue taxes and interest.[31]

An article on the decline of the company's stock price reviewed the major events since August 2003 to August 2004 during which time the share price went from $5.56 to $1.49. The dreary losses were brought up, the large debt was discussed, the issuance of a further 29 million shares (giving the bank lenders control) was mentioned. A professor at Le Moyne College stated, "Oneida's problems result from its inefficiencies and poor management. It appears by some of its actions the company has taken—such as failing to make contributions to its pension plan—that Oneida remains in need of cash. The possibility of a Chapter 11 bankruptcy reorganization under court protection remains."[32]

The Oneida board of directors was officially rearranged late in October with the resignations of the majority of its members. Those departing included Executive Vice President Allan Conseur whose resignation led to a highly lucrative consultancy for the company in the form of "Project

Virtual"—a euphemism for outsourcing high-end flatware that had once been produced at the Sherrill factory.[33]

Six replacement board members would stand for election at the company's next annual meeting, May 25, 2005. "We are extremely pleased to welcome these new members," Pete Kallet enthused. As he saw it, their diversity, talents, and perspectives would be "of great benefit to Oneida's operations as the company moves forward and continues to build its business for the future." Among these new diverse and talented executives was Terry G. Westbrook who would soon take over from Kallet as President and CEO with Kallet remaining as denatured Chairman of the Board until the next annual meeting.[34]

The dismal year spun itself out. A new Chief Financial Officer was hired; the factory and its remaining 500 jobs would close in three phases; 400 other jobs were to remain in the Oneida/Sherrill area. Outsourcing was proceeding on schedule and a deal was struck with glassmaker Anchor Hocking to consolidate and co-brand the foodservice glassware lines of the two companies. "This collaboration," Senior Vice President Jim Joseph happily noted, "is an ideal way for Oneida to build on our strategy to offer total tabletop solutions."

As of December, Oneida had sent closure notices to its remaining factory employees but had not advised them as to severance payment. 60% of the workers affected were 50 years or older and understandably anxious. The company was losing less money—$23.8 million for the third quarter although revenues were down compared to the same quarter a year earlier. On December 11th, it was reported that the company would pay $1.2 million in severance pay to 450 factory employees. "Our future performance will benefit from ongoing internal improvements," Kallet observed as the year dragged to a close. The new CFO spoke of "rationalizing our business model and maximizing shareholder value." Among those experiencing such rationalization was Dave Gymburch. It had been his unhappy job to dutifully report to the press and public the depressing news about Oneida Ltd.'s declining fortunes over recent years and put as good a face on things as possible. He did this with dexterity and grace and, when he left, there wasn't much more to say.[35]

As the company's fiscal performance declined, so too did the impact of its once powerful brand recognition. The Oneida name was devalued by being placed into Wal-Mart and other large discount contexts. It was devalued further by being placed on products imported by Oneida from eastern Asia. Both situations tended to undermine the power of the trademark with the consuming public and regular retail trade. Also reducing the impact of the Oneida name was the decline in advertising expenditure and the attempt to get advertising space through product barter. This latter led to a loss of quality control over advertising appearance in terms of publications used and page-position therein. Cheapening the Oneida name in this fashion, commentator Rob Frankel noted, was brand suicide. "This is what happens when corporate management have no idea about how strongly the brands their fathers built are undermined by quick licensing agreements."[36] The head of a New York City ad agency added, "What's unacceptable is how Oneida Ltd. has fallen out of the public's awareness. They used to do some stunning advertising. But recently, I just haven't seen any."

The Sherrill factory, with its equipment and supplies, was sold in early 2005 to two former employees of Oneida Ltd. who previously had managed the plant. A new entity, Sherrill Manufacturing, had been created and given a grant of $350,000 by New York State whose governor said that eventually $1.9 million would be invested in the business. $165,000 of this money went to purchase the factory which, initially, would employ 100 people to make some flatware for Oneida Ltd. while looking to diversify into other products. Oneida Ltd. kept all its flatware trademarks and designs.[37]

Pete Kallet's resignation came in March. He was to hang on as board chairman until the annual meeting in May and was then to become "vice chairman of strategic alliances and corporate development." He would continue on the payroll for another couple of years until July 2007 at his reduced salary of $300,000. He would also be eligible for "bonuses" up to $85,000 and reimbursements of $25,000 for "unspecified expenses."[38]

That spring, Oneida closed its Buffalo distribution center at a cost of $3 million, claiming that the products could be moved from other locations. The next item of liquidation coming to public attention was Pete Kallet's personal "moving sale." When asked what was being sold, those conducting the sale for Kallet "became uncooperative, noting that *The [Oneida Daily] Dispatch* would not be covering the garage sale if it was being held by someone else. They also asked that no items be named."[39]

Oneida Ltd.'s loss for fiscal year 2004, according to the company's new president and CEO, Terry Westbrook, amounted to $51.5 million on reduced revenues of $20 million in the fourth quarter and included one-time expenses of $25.2 million.[40] This was a considerable improvement over the previous year's loss of $99.2 million despite including impairment losses of $37 million on depreciable and intangible assets.

Peter Kallet's last gesture as an Oneida Ltd. executive was putting his name along with that of his boss, Mr. Westbrook, on the stockholders letter in the fiscal 2005 annual report and on the accompanying proxy statement. The latter document invited shareholders to the annual meeting now to be held in Chicago, not the Mansion House in Oneida where it had been held the previous 123 times. At that meeting, base pay for board members was raised from $19,000 to $36,000 along with new financial incentives to attend board meetings.

Loss in the second quarter of 2005 came to $6.76 million, in the third quarter, $6 million. Customers were dropping out due to worry over supply or, themselves, turning to direct import. Gross profits were back up to 36% thanks to 100% imported product. However, 23 company stores were closed, product lines were discontinued, and net loss came to $16.1 million for the first nine months. Bankruptcy proceedings under Chapter 11 would commence on March 14, 2006.[41]

***

Inquiring into why Oneida Ltd. closed its factory, one newspaper analyst reviewed corporate strategy since 1996 which centered around the decision to sell a complete range of tabletop products. Much blame was laid upon a sluggish economy topped off by the terrorist attacks of 9/11/01 and its impact on the company's sales. "When the economy is not doing well, those marginal companies suffer the most," a Cornell finance professor pointed out.[42]

That was true of Oneida Ltd. For the middle years of the 1990s, it had had good net income, by historical standards, of between 4 and 6%. Fiscal year 2000 featured the Libbey takeover attempt which had followed a large investment by Oneida in consumer dinnerware and commercial glassware. Net income plunged to $5.5 million or 1.1% of net sales. This poor result came to pass due to $44.3 million worth of restructuring costs which included the $18.3 million Libbey lawsuit defense, $12 million of asset impairment, topped off by $11 million of operation restructuring costs, and $3 million of inventory write-downs. The next year, fiscal 2001, would show a net loss of $1.3 million thanks to a significant drop in gross profit percentage, an inventory write-down of $24 million, and an increase in interest expense of around $11 million.

Thus the stage was set for disaster as the company took on additional long-term debt due to its acquisition binge in the amount of $184,320,000 in the same year, thereby raising this level of debt by 187%. Long-term debt now exceeded stockholders equity by $158,507,000 or 127%. A basic economic rule of thumb is that, when total liabilities exceed stockholders equity, the creditors actually control the business. As for total liabilities, they now stood at $486,265,000 or 292% above stockholders equity.

Even in good times with outstanding profits, acquiring debt alone of this dimension would have been poor business judgment by a manufacturer of low-tech, consumer durables facing rising import competition. The urgent necessity to pay down this debt would soon enough sap the company's ability to maintain its strength in such areas as product development, equipment maintenance, capital spending, and advertising. No time and wherewithal was left to work out a new destiny for this rugged old company that had meant so much to so many for so long. For 125 years the company had a goodly heritage. Husbanding its resources, the executives of Oneida propelled the company to leadership of its industry and provided for company survival in hard times.

The times considered in this book were, to be sure, complicated and challenging. But everyone must wonder: How much of the blame for failure can be attributed to the real people who made actual decisions? About 91% of business failures are due to "management incompetence," a category including the effects of recessions and unfavorable industry trends. "This placement is logical," business economist Eugene Brigham notes, "since managements should plan ahead and be prepared for both booms and recessions. Financial difficulties are usually the result of a series of errors, misjudgments and interrelated weaknesses which can be attributed directly or indirectly to management and signs of potential financial distress are often evident before the firm actually fails."[43]

Notes to Chapter 7

1   Linda Murphy, "Growth: A personal professional goal for Kallet," *Utica Observer-Dispatch*, November 1, 1998.

2   Oneida Ltd. Annual Report for Fiscal Year Ending January 29, 2000 ("unusual charges," 28).
3   "Oneida Broadens Strategic Restructuring Program, Expects Improved Performance, Reduced Costs," Oneida Ltd. press release, March 31, 1999.
4   Oneida Ltd. Annual Report for Fiscal Years Ending January 29, 2000, 13, and January 27, 2001, 2-3.
5   "Oneida Ltd. to Acquire Viners in U. K.; Expands International Distribution Rights in Separate Transaction," Oneida Ltd. press release, May 30, 2000.
6   "Oneida Ltd. to Acquire Sakura, Inc.; Will Accelerate Growth in Consumer Dinnerware," Oneida Ltd. press release, May 23, 2000.
7   "Oneida Ltd. To Acquire Delco International; Strategic Acquisition Expands Foodservice Division," Oneida Ltd. press release, March 31, 2000; Charley Hannagan, "Oneida Ltd. cuts income in restated earnings," *Syracuse Post-Standard*, December 7, 2002
8   Oneida Ltd. Annual Report for Years Ending January 27, 2001, 18, 21, and January 26, 2002, 30-32.
9   Oneida Ltd. Annual Report for Year Ending January 27, 2001, 15.
10 Oneida Ltd. Proxy Statement, April 24, 2001, 6.
11 Charley Hannagan, "Oneida Ltd. says earnings will fall short," *Syracuse Post-Standard*, May 1, 2001.
12 Ginny Freebern, "Communication Day 9/26/01," internal email to Oneida Ltd. employees in the author's possession.
13 "Communication Day: October 30, 2001," *The Oneida Silversmith*, Fall 2001, 2-3.
14 Oneida Ltd. Annual Report for Fiscal Year Ending January 26, 2002, 32.
15 Oneida Ltd. Annual Report for Years Ending January 26, 2002, 21, 30, and January 31, 2004, 12.
16 Jolene Walters, "Oneida Ltd. sees profits rise in 2002," *Oneida Daily Dispatch*, November 15, 2002.
17 Oneida Ltd. Annual Report for Fiscal Years Ending January 26, 2002, 17, and January 25, 2003, 19.
18 Oneida Ltd. Annual Report for Fiscal Year Ending January 25, 2003, 9, 19.
19 Oneida Ltd. Annual Report for Fiscal Year Ending January 31, 2004, 19, 40.
20 Oneida Ltd. Annual Report for Fiscal Year Ending January 25, 2003, 2.
21 Oneida Ltd. Proxy Statement, April 30, 2004, 11; Oneida Ltd. Annual Report for Fiscal Year Ending January 25, 2003, 26; Oneida Ltd. Prosy Statement, April 25, 2003, 8.

22 Marreca Fiore, "Analysts: Oneida Ltd. will do OK in long term," *Utica Observer-Dispatch*, December 7, 2002; Charley Hannagan, "Oneida Looks to Regain Shine," *Syracuse Post-Standard*, March 19, 2004.
23 Kurt Wanfried, "Oneida Ltd. to close 5 factories," *Oneida Daily Dispatch*, November 1, 2003; Staff, "Oneida Ltd. plant at risk," *Utica Observer-Dispatch*, December 5, 2003; R. Patrick Corbett and Marrecca Fiore, "Efficiency key to Oneida Ltd. survival," *Utica Observer-Dispatch*, December 7, 2003.
24 Chana R. Schoenberger, "Tarnished," *Forbes*, March 15, 2004, taken from: http://biz.yahoo.com/fo/040226/56ab9e57dc1b4556984c014cd8583a32_1.html; Kurt Wanfried and Jolene Walters, "Websites analyze Oneida Ltd. woes," *Oneida Daily Dispatch*, March 4, 2004; "Our view: Many paying price for company's miscalculation," *Oneida Daily Dispatch*, April 3, 2004; Charley Hannagan, "Oneida Looks to Regain Shine," *Syracuse Post-Standard*, March 19, 2004.
25 Oneida Ltd. Annual Report for Fiscal Year Ending January 31, 2004, "To Our Shareholders" (second unnumbered page).
26 Oneida Ltd. Annual Report for Fiscal Year Ending January 31, 2004; Oneida Ltd. Proxy Statement, April 30, 2004, 9.
27 Dan Guzewich, "Trouble at Oneida Ltd. table," *Rome Daily Sentinel*, May 27, 2004; Jolene Walters, "Oneida Ltd. leaders face shareholder questions," *Oneida Daily Dispatch*, May 27, 2004.
28 Charley Hannagan, "Lenders to take control of Oneida Ltd.," *Syracuse Post-Standard*, June 26, 2004; Kurt Wanfried, "Oneida Ltd., lenders strike tentative deal," *Oneida Daily Dispatch*, June 26, 2004; Traci Gregory, "Bank control part of Oneida Ltd. deal," *Utica Observer-Dispatch*, July 13, 2004.
29 Charley Hannagan, "Oneida Ltd. to close Sherrill Factory," *Syracuse Post-Standard*, September 10, 2004; Jolene Walters, "Oneida Ltd. to close Sherrill plant," *Oneida Daily Dispatch*, September 10, 2004; Jolene Walters, "Kallet says plant will never reopen," *Oneida Daily Dispatch*, September 11, 2004.
30 Kurt Wanfried, "Oneida Ltd. launches 'Project Virtual,'" *Oneida Daily Dispatch*, September 17, 2004.
31 Charley Hannagan, "Pension agency files lien against Oneida," *Syracuse Post-Standard*, September 23, 2004.
32 Charley Hannagan, "Lost Silver Lining," *Syracuse Post-Standard*, September 27, 2004.
33 Charley Hannagan, "Some Oneida executives took pay cuts," *Syracuse Post Standard*, September 16, 2004.

34 Kurt Wanfried, "Oneida Ltd. shakes up board," *Oneida Daily Dispatch*, October 27, 2004.
35 "Oneida Ltd. and Anchor Hocking Announce Licensing Agreement for Foodservice Glassware," Oneida Ltd. Press Release, November 14, 2004; Charley Hannagan, "Oneida sends closure notices to employees," *Syracuse Post-Standard*, December 2, 2004; Staff, "Oneida Ltd. losing less money, closing some stores," *Syracuse Post-Standard*, December 11, 2004; Charley Hannagan, "Oneida begins series of phased layoffs, *Syracuse Post-Standard*, January 27, 2005.
36 Traci Gregory, "Outsourcing may tarnish Oneida," *Utica Observer-Dispatch*, February 3, 2005.
37 Jacques Picard, "Oneida Ltd. factory finds a buyer," *Oneida Daily Dispatch*, February 16, 2005; Staff, "Property Transfers," *Oneida Daily Dispatch*, May 18, 2005.
38 Tim Knauss, "Oneida Ltd. CEO Kallet resigns his posts," *Syracuse Post-Standard*, March 24, 2005; James T. Mulder, "Oneida to keep paying ex-CEO's salary, expenses," *Syracuse Post-Standard*, March 31, 2005; Kurt Wanfried, "Kallet retires as Oneida Ltd. chairman," *Oneida Daily Dispatch*, May 26, 2005.
39 Staff, "Oneida Ltd. to close Buffalo distribution center," *Syracuse Post-Standard*, April 13, 2005; Penny Stickney and Wayne Myers, "Kallet holds 'moving sale,'" *Oneida Daily Dispatch*, April 23, 2005.
40 Staff, "Oneida Ltd. posts loss of $51 million," *Utica Observer-Dispatch*, April 16, 2005.
41 Oneida Ltd. Annual Report for Fiscal Year Ending January 29, 2005; Oneida Ltd. Proxy Statement, April 29, 2005; Associated Press, "Oneida reports $51M loss for fiscal 2005," *Syracuse Post-Standard*, April 16, 2005.
42 Charley Hannagan, "Why Oneida Ltd. closed its last U.S. factory," *Syracuse Post-Standard*, September 12, 2004.
43 Eugene F. Brigham, *Financial Management: Theory and Practice* (Dryden Press, Hinsdale, Ill., 1977), 787.

8

Epilogue: Bankruptcy and Beyond

An emaciated Oneida Ltd. limped into late 2005 claiming an operating income of $3 million as compared with the net loss of $16.1 million for the same nine month period of 2004. Full year results for fiscal 2007 (twelve months ending in February) were not reported. However, on March 9, 2006, a letter was forthcoming from Terry Westbrook, now president of the corporation, announcing that financial progress had been limited by the legacy debt burden despite hard work "to develop a plan to restructure the balance sheet." Therefore, the company had struck a deal with its lenders "to recapitalize the company through a pre-negotiated Chapter 11 proceeding." The entire process was expected to take only 90 days at which point Oneida Ltd. would exit bankruptcy. "Stakeholders," that is, suppliers, customers and business partners would not be affected.

Shareholders would be another matter. They, of course, would be wiped out. Westbrook went on to say, "For over 100 years [slight hyperbole] Oneida has been an industry leader and we believe will continue to be a leader for many years to come."[1] Employees, retirees, neighbors, and friends might have wondered—leaders of what industry? The industry that Oneida once led actually manufactured product—this being the normal function of "industry." There did not seem to be any "industry" of this sort left.

Debt, it further reported, would be reduced by $100 million. All outstanding common stock would be "cancelled and receive no recovery and new common stock would be issued to holders of its debt." Otherwise, it would be business as usual as far as the employees and suppliers were concerned. A spokesman was quoted as helpfully explaining, "The business has been performing quite well over the past year, but they've got a very large debt load for a company of their size." Once out of bankruptcy,

Oneida was "to receive another $40 million of credit financing" and $170 million of long term financing." With its bankruptcy filing, the company listed debts of $333.2 million against assets of $305.3 million.[2]

It came out as part of the bankruptcy deal that the company's pension plan was under funded by $40 million. The company wished to terminate further payments into the fund and have the federal pension insurer, the Pension Benefit Guaranty Corporation, take over the plan.

There was, briefly, a committee of Equity Holders who appealed to a federal judge to be made official outside overseers of the company's bankruptcy proceedings. The Creditor Committee appointed on April 10th was said to be unwilling to look after shareholder interests, especially as creditors expected 100% recovery of money owed to them. Also, the Equity Holders Committee believed the pre-negotiated bankruptcy plan was marred by self-dealing. A hearing was set for May 1st. Apparently, the court agreed to recognize the Equity Holders Committee which then insisted that Oneida Ltd. could be sold for $330 million. This would be enough money to pay off lenders, creditors and provide something for shareholders.

Company management said they had tried three times to sell the company without success before proceeding to bankruptcy. They appealed to experts who said the company might fetch $230 to $243 million. In the course of all this, a newspaper report of July 12 revealed a restatement of the corporation's refinancing: $118 million of secured debt to be refinanced, $107 million of reorganized stock to other holders of secured debt, $15 million to unsecured debtors, and $3 million to the Federal Pension Benefit Guaranty Corporation.

Now hedge funds became interested. It seems two Oneida lenders had a large position in reorganized Oneida stock with one fund thus owning 29.5% of the company. Oneida's management claimed to be cheered by this development. Their plans for the bankrupt company must be working, they reasoned, if hedge funds thought the company worth buying. At least one reporter following these developments suspected that these outfits planned to strip the company down and, after a period of time, make a bundle by selling it via an initial public offering.[3]

Then came the announcement that Oneida Ltd. had agreed to be sold. The creditors' plan died aborning as two hedge funds—D.E. Shaw Laminar Portfolios and Xerion Capital Partners—came forward with an offer of $222.5 million (about $100 million less than the company's total debt). After Oneida signed a letter of intent, the only thing remaining was to secure approval of the sale by the federal bankruptcy court. Along with paying off secured and unsecured bank claims and creditors, the offer was said to "include an element of consideration" for the company's "common equity holders." The original shareholders having been wiped out by the Chapter 11 bankruptcy, this latter statement must have referred to the new-found "reorganized" shareholders.

This development was cause for congratulations all around. The intended sale was taken to mean that the company had made great progress after closing its factories and becoming a purveyor solely of imported merchandise. Jim Joseph, Oneida's new president as of June, said the sale "would set the table for Oneida's growth." A Mr. Christopher Smith, now Oneida's chairman, claimed that the purchase by two hedge funds "represents a very favorable outcome for, among other parties, Oneida's employees."[4] Joseph may have been less sure about that to judge by the fact that his contract with Oneida called for an annual base salary of $300,000, a signing bonus, a cash incentive plan—and payment of moving expenses.

After all the attention garnered by the proposed purchase by the hedge funds, the federal court favored the lender-approved reorganization plan as the quickest and best way for Oneida to get out of bankruptcy. Joseph asserted that Oneida "would emerge with the best balance sheet in the industry, the best brand and best management team." The judge having approved the pre-negotiated plan, the company expected to be out of bankruptcy around September 12th.[5]

In April, it was reported that Oneida was penalized $293,760 in 2005 for having failed to increase employment by an amount agreed at the time the company accepted a job creation grant. In May when a company director was reported as saying (the humor apparently unintentional): "If the company didn't have to pay interest on its debt, it would have been profitable in 2006."

Despite revenues dropping to $350.8 million, operational income was up to $12.1 million. Fiscal year 2006 net loss was $21.9 million compared to $51 million the year before. Another 150 jobs were to be lost when Oneida decided, in July, to close its new $6 million, 205,000 square-foot distribution center in Sherrill and move warehousing to Savannah, Georgia, to save shipping costs from the Orient and elsewhere. Marketing activities had already been consolidated in New York City. This left perhaps 200 employees at Oneida.[6]

There were only a few details to be tidied up as calendar year 2006 progressed. The Federal Pension Benefit Guaranty Corporation in early September took over Oneida's 31% funded pension plan. This arrangement would, for workers aged 65, pay a maximum of $47,659, a figure which Oneida's recently retired executives might have found contemptibly low. International Wire, which had previously bought the Camden Wire Company from Oneida, now purchased, in early November, part of Oneida's former Knife Plant for $600,000. After a further investment of $14 million, this company planned to make bare copper wire at the facility to complement its other wire factories in the local area. This provided a satisfying sense of irony to those reminded of the sale of Camden Wire by Oneida Ltd.

And as for Oneida Ltd., it announced a new board of directors "carefully chosen for their keen perspective," according to a *Post-Standard* article in November. Extremely pleased with the new group, Joseph claimed that "icons like them have the luxury of picking and choosing what boards they serve on and they've chosen us."

The company was never required to publish any financial results after it became privately owned. As time passed, it became difficult to track the works of Oneida and its icons in subsequent years as newspaper coverage declined. The little one could glean from the press included these items.

After bailing out of its pension obligations by turning it over to the Federal Pension Benefit Guaranty Corporation, Oneida decided to sue that agency. After the plan turnover, the company was required by law to pay a fee of $1,250 a year for three years for each of the 1,900 workers and retirees covered by the plan. This came to $6.9 million which Oneida said should be part of the company's *unsecured* claims which were dismissed by the court-approved reorganization plan. It almost seemed as though Oneida wanted one last chance at reneging.[7]

In February 2008, the company sold its Australian holdings for an unknown amount of money despite that business being very successful, according to CEO Jim Joseph. He went on to say that licensing of Oneida brands would be an important source of growth for Oneida.

Having sold its Buffalo China operations to private investors for $5.5 million in 2004, Oneida agreed to buy a minimum amount of product from the new owners, who, in turn, would not compete with Oneida. Apparently, Oneida found it cheaper to buy Asian china rather than Buffalo-made china and did not live up to the minimum purchase agreement. Buffalo had signed a five-year non-compete agreement with Oneida which that company then violated by selling to Oneida's customer, Outback Steakhouse. Thus, a mutual violation took place.

A judge ordered Oneida to pay Buffalo $1.9 million for the non-purchase violation and Buffalo to pay Oneida $800,000 for the non-compete infraction. "It made more financial sense for us to pay the penalty," Joseph said although Oneida was the loser by $1.1 million. One of Buffalo's owners said both sides were "winners" and would "continue to do business with each other." Maybe Buffalo looked forward to a few more "winning" deals before the five-year agreement ran out in 2009?[8]

There was some unrest among Oneida's pensioners concerning the use of company stock to fund its pension plan. The stock so used became worthless upon the company's bankruptcy. A class action law suit announced in May 2007 claimed a value of $14.7 million for this stock which the company's directors should have sold timely knowing the company was heading for bankruptcy. One of the litigants said he was not after the money the lawsuit might provide. Rather, he wanted "to get answers about how a once vital company could fall into bankruptcy." "We were lied to for so long," that individual added, "we just want to know what really went on."

In August 2007, the press stated that a judge would decide whether Oneida "must pay millions of dollars in 'termination fees' to the government's pension insurer." The following May, a federal judge cleared the way for former Oneida Ltd. employees to continue their class-action law suit against the directors of the company's employee stock ownership plan.[9] This may be one reason why former Oneida directors have been tight-lipped with me when asked about what happened.

In early January of 2009, the company announced the remaining 20 factory or "Home" stores would be closed by the end of April due to a very tough retail environment. The possibility was held out that stores in Sherrill, N. Y., and Niagara Falls, Canada, would reopen at year end. In the meantime, a liquidator had been hired to sell out existing store inventories. Money spent on the store operation would be reallocated to what Joseph described as "our global Foodservice initiative, Internet fulfillment business, and the pursuit of worldwide licensing opportunities."

The year 2009 also saw Oneida turning over what once were its "crown jewels" to Robinson Knife Co., who, by the end of March, would attend to all Oneida retail sales. Robinson would pay royalties to Oneida on such retail sales and Oneida would retain "intellectual property rights" to its brand names (Oneida, Community, etc.) and designs now being sold by the knife company. What Oneida would not retain were about 75 people no longer needed as a result of this maneuver. The new-found source of royalties would be used to pay down debt. The personnel reduction would leave Oneida with a total workforce of 525 people of which 140 would be located in central New York versus the 3,200 employees of 1996.[10]

In November 2011, Jim Joseph was delighted to announce that Oneida Ltd. had been sold to Monomoy Capital Management, a New York City-based equity fund that owned Anchor Hocking, a long established Ohio-based glassware manufacturer. He said that dealing with a single owner rather than "a handful of banks and hedge funds" and the addition of a line of Anchor Hocking products to Oneida's offerings was a "home run" that should add another 130 years to Oneida's existence. Monomoy management was equally excited about landing the "iconic" Oneida brands.[11]

Joseph also spoke of selling Oneida Ltd. and Anchor Hocking products to department stores in the country. How this prospect will fit in with Oneida's 2009 deal with Robinson Knife to sell Oneida flatware in the United States and pay royalties to Oneida was not explained. Perhaps the "multiyear" arrangement with the knife company has come to an end.

The lead article in the *New York Times* business section on January 6, 2012 (which landed up on the front page of the *Syracuse Post-Standard* two days later), had to do with Oneida Ltd. making a comeback in the consumer flatware business. It seems the new owners of Oneida Ltd. wanted to expand the business for which they are said to have paid $100 million. A potted history of the company, replete with several errors, included no mention of the increase in long-term debt in the summer of 2000 to $282 million from $98.5 million the year before. The majority of this borrowed money was used to pay for three overpriced acquisitions—two importers of cheap flatware and one importer of dinnerware. This new borrowing was made up largely of "good will" (i.e., hot air) and, when not paid on time, resulted in waivers of payment, increased interest rates, asset stripping and, ultimately, the bankruptcy of the company.

Joseph said that Monomoy Capital is not a "strip and flip" firm. A Mr. Collin of Monomoy said he hoped "to strengthen Oneida so that within five years it can be sold or taken public again."

We shall see.

The Allen family was always prominent in Oneida Community affairs and then in the management of its successor, Oneida Ltd. After the latter's bankruptcy, Wilbur Allen continued as head of personnel and it was his unhappy duty to terminate people from the remnant company payroll which began at about 2000 local people in 2007 and gradually shrank to around 70 by June 2012. His last 13 firings occurred on January 8th, 2012, after which he was himself dismissed by the current Oneida management. Cold-blooded OCQ.

Although the parking lot behind the former Oneida administration building contains progressively fewer automobiles, the residential street outside suffers increasing numbers of tractor trailers serving International Wire which rumble through the once-quiet Kenwood neighborhood on their way to Oneida's former knife plant, now also a part of this successful company's "Camden Wire" division.

Dominating the north wall and overlooking the long boardroom table of Oneida Ltd.'s administration building is a large and stunning braiding by Jessie Kinsley (1858-1938). Born in the Oneida Community, she became a superb fabric artist whose unique creations have been displayed in many museums over many years. They all have a theme and illuminate a story, biblical passage, poem or just a memorable phrase. Her boardroom braiding was inspired by the company's then new and grandiose 1926 headquarters.

Local scenes border a woven map of North America, the Atlantic Ocean, and British Isles and include representations of the Mansion House, the Administration Building, factories, fields and the hills that form the Oneida Valley. On the map itself are again positioned the Mansion House and Administration Building along with the Canadian factories and Oneida's plant in Sheffield, England. Jessie Kinsley's title for this magnificent work is "Memory Hither Come" from a poem by William Blake.

We shall remember.

Notes to Epilogue

1   Staff, "Oneida Ltd. sees income of $3 million," *Oneida Daily Dispatch*, October 29, 2005; Terry G. Westbrook, to "All Present and Future Oneida Ltd. Retirees," letter dated March 9, 2006.
2   "The business had been performing quite well" is from James T. Mulder, "Oneida Ltd. to reorganize under Chapter 11," *Syracuse Post-Standard*, March

11, 2006; Associated Press, "Negotiated Bankruptcy: Oneida Ltd. hopes for quick Chapter 11 reorganization," *Syracuse Post-Standard*, March 21, 2006.
3   Charley Hannagan, "Teetering Oneida cuts net loss in half," *Syracuse Post Standard*, May 5, 2006; Charley Hannagan, "Court to hear Oneida dispute," *Syracuse Post-Standard*, July 12, 2006; the reporter "following these developments" was Charley Hannagan, "Hedge funds bid for bankrupt Oneida," *Syracuse Post-Standard*, July 14, 2006.
4   Kurt Wanfried, "Oneida Ltd. agrees to sale," *Oneida Daily Dispatch*, July 17, 2006.
5   Staff, "Oneida Ltd. to go private Sept. 12," *Oneida Daily Dispatch*, September 2, 2006; Cynthia Ward Vesey, "Oneida Primed to Exit Ch. 11," *HomeWorld Business*, July-31-August 13, 2006 (vol. 18, no. 16).
6   Mike Andrews, "Lack of new jobs leads to state fine," *Syracuse Post-Standard*, April 20, 2006; Charley Hannagan, "Teetering Oneida cuts net loss in half," *Syracuse Post-Standard*, May 5, 2006; Charley Hannagan, "Oneida Ltd. to move warehouse to Georgia," *Syracuse Post-Standard*, July 27, 2006.
7   Jeannine Aversa, "Federal agency takes Oneida Ltd. pension plan," *Syracuse Post-Standard*, September 7, 2006; Leanne Root, "International Wire buys knife plant," *Oneida Daily Dispatch*, November 2, 2006; Dee Klees, "Oneida names board," *Syracuse Post-Standard*, November 11, 2006; Patrick Fitzgerald, "Oneida Ltd. files suit against pension agency," *Syracuse Post-Standard*, November 17, 2006.
8   Anon., "Oneida Ltd. to sell business in Australia," *Syracuse Post-Standard*, February 28, 2008; Charley Hannagan, "Niagara, Oneida settle; both pay," *Syracuse Post-Standard*, April 3, 2008.
9   Charley Hannagan, "Oneida workers sue over stock-plan decline," *Syracuse Post-Standard*, May 18, 2007; Anon., "Judge to rule on Oneida dispute over pension fees," *Syracuse Post-Standard*, August 1, 2007; Charley Hannagan, "Judge allows lawsuit by ex-Oneida workers," *Syracuse Post-Standard*, May 10, 2008.
10 Staff, "Oneida Limited closing all 20 stores," *Oneida Daily Dispatch*, January 8, 2009; Charley Hannagan, "Oneida Ltd. in marketing deal," *Syracuse Post-Standard*, January 28, 2009; Lynn Collier, "Oneida Ltd. contracts out sales in U.S.," *Oneida Daily Dispatch*, January 30, 2009.
11 Charles McChesney, "Oneida Ltd. sold to equity fund," *Syracuse Post-Standard*, November 4, 2011; Caitlin Traynor, "Oneida Ltd. joins Monomoy," *Oneida Daily Dispatch*, November 8, 2011.

Addendums

Appendix 1
The Need for Diversification

The ultimate failure of Oneida Ltd to diversify its factory and earnings base in addition to poor management of its existing businesses brought its extinction after 125 years of existence.

May 1, 1972
P. T. Noyes
Oneida Ltd. Strategic Situation and the Search for Alternatives

Dear Pete,

Last week you raised the central issue (in my mind) of our recent Management Planning Committee (MPC) meetings.

You will recall the graph issued at the last MPC meeting which showed our projected sales through 1977, the rise and fall of the rate of family formation through 1982 and the probable end of tariff quota in the autumn of 1976. You will also remember that in 1971, stainless flatware (domestic) accounted for $4,166,866 of our total U.S. profits of $4,391,710. Our ROI on stainless was 11.6% against an overall ROI of 6.79%.

Given the tariff quota, we have somewhat over four years to earn sufficient money to enable us to either significantly expand other existing lines (e.g. sterling and holloware) and/or develop new business by acquisition or product development to replace the probable loss of domestic stainless volume. There may be a third kind of alternative and that would be to beef up our import program with a view to being able to quickly switch our consumer stainless sales to foreign merchandise on a post-tariff situation. This might allow us to maintain sales dollars but profit dollars might be another thing. And, the effect upon our manufacturing/employment posture would be profound.

Perhaps none of this will come to pass. Perhaps we'll be able to improve our methods and productivity to the point where we can become competitive with stainless flatware produced anywhere in the world. If we think so, we can go on as we are, but in my view we would be playing a form of Russian Roulette and the risks in that game are too high despite the favorable odds.

Furthermore, I believe we must commit the necessary resources of time, talent and money now if we are to have viable product alternatives at hand by 1977. If we wait, we may find ourselves trying to develop solutions to our dilemma under circumstances of real duress—a dwindling profit position, a foreshortened time frame, declining employment, increasing difficulty in selling what we make and the consummate need to learn how and where to diversify along with the immediate opportunity to do so.

If you believe that we are faced with such a strategic threat than the present allocation of resources becomes even more pressing. How much money (earnings, debt or whatever) should be spent on existing alternatives—holloware and sterling? How much on new alternatives—product development and acquisition? Regarding the latter, if you believe we will need product alternatives not presently known to us, then it is my feeling that we need top management time and talent given to the subject on a continuing and urgent basis. I am not advocating a wild course of high hopes and wild spending. But I do urge a course of close analysis and deliberate action and this in itself will require money in addition to the previously mentioned commitment of time and talent by top people.

I realize that you and others may or may not agree with the above view of our future situation. Also, I appreciate that if you should be in more or less agreement, that you need a consensus of MPC personnel to begin to "invent" a different future on the basis of present action. In any event, I believe we should somehow arrive at some articulated, management-backed statement of our future strategic situation. Whatever this statement may be will then determine what we do—continue to evolve as we are or look for new departures or both.

Sincerely,

J. L. Hatcher

ONEIDA (COMMUNITY) LIMITED

October 25, 1984
TO: R. E. Sanderson
SUBJECT: <u>DIVERSIFICATION</u>

Dear Bob,

The attached memo results from the planning meetings we have held this year. However, it deals with a problem that has waxed and waned for years—the fact that our major flatware can be produced equally well and at much less cost in other parts of the world due to reasons beyond our control. It is a great credit to our company that we have fought off this inexorable fact as long and as well as we have.

With the advent of famous old sterling manufacturers as importers of high quality stainless under their own names, designed and manufactured to their standards and supported by their established marketing practices, the nature of the competition has changed dramatically and we begin to lose some of the natural advantages we enjoy over normal importers.

In any case, in our people and our community, we have not only a societal commitment to protect but an asset of great strength as long as there is appropriate work to be done. It is our job to see that this commitment is continued and that this asset is properly used and that these hands "be not idle." The purpose of this memo is to begin a dialogue on the subject with a view toward arriving at a dedicated and orchestrated program to achieve success in this most essential matter. We have in time past been able to put off the evil day because something always seemed to turn up—tariff protection, quality upgrading, unique marketing efforts, competitor inattention—but now we can no longer do so.

Sincerely,

[signed "Lang"]
J. L. Hatcher

cc: J. L. Marcellus, H. C. Lilholt, W. E. Wild

JOHN P. L. HATCHER

TRAPS TO TABLEWARE TO ? (1984)

The Current Problem

At our most recent Long Range Planning meetings we tentatively completed Corporate Strategy statements and then began to get into general Corporate Objectives. It is the fourth point under this latter heading that I would like to develop in this memo: "To develop and market products that are compatible with the silversmith's technology, skills, organizational structure and facilities to provide future employment security." In my view, this is the single greatest corporate challenge that we presently face.

The managements of Camden Wire and Buffalo China are quite confident that the means and methodology are at hand for them to become the lowest cost producers of their particular product lines (although Buffalo would add that certain countries, with whom they compete, pay no attention to cost when pricing their product). Most importantly, both of these companies pay virtually the same price as anyone else in the world for their raw material.

It is this latter fact that compromises the Silversmiths Division. Stainless steel represents about 31% of our total cost and we pay between 32% and 45% more for it than our Far Eastern competitors. With all the method improvement we can foresee, it is unlikely that we shall be able to reduce direct labor—now 14.5% of our total cost—sufficiently to make us competitive with Oriental product. Also, at present, Korean and Japanese direct wage rates are 10% and 50% respectively of ours. Although we may be able to reduce in dollar terms that 55% of our costs represented by overhead, it seems unlikely that we shall be able to save sufficient money in this area to make us competitive in either price or profits with overseas competitors. Despite any reduction in overhead spending, as volume declines, we may expect the percentage of cost represented by overhead to remain the same or go up. We know there are people in this world who produce stainless flatware that is as well made and designed as ours and do it for less money.

It is interesting to note how reduced unit volumes have apparently affected the percentage composition of costs since 1975. All figures are unofficial.

1983 Factory Costs - Average Percentage (all figures are unofficial; SS = stainless steel)

	Material	Labor	Overhead
Current Community SS patterns	30.3	14.5	55.2
Current Oneida Deluxe SS patterns	31.2	14.7	54.1
1975 SS lines	37.9	15.2	46.8

Historical Background

As a replacement for animal traps—the product that saved the Oneida Community in the 19th century and provided the means and money to develop the flatware business in the 20th—tableware has served us well. We now need something to begin to replace tableware in the same way.

Tableware may well remain an important product for the corporation into the indefinite future. However, its seems likely that market forces will continue to force us to make less at home and import more from abroad. For about 30 years, we have recognized the possibility of producing year by year, less tableware units. And, as a company, we have made various attempts at diversification.

In the 1950s, when silverplate declined, we sought a government jet blade contract to tide us over while we developed stainless steel flatware (really a product line extension, not a diversification) and melamine dinnerware. In the 1960s, with the demand for stainless flatware expanding rapidly, we extended our range of design and quality, sought tariff protection from Import and installed overseas plants. In the 1970s, we began to buy successful non-tableware businesses, which while successfully broadening our sales and earnings base, did not help us use our Sherrill facilities except as such acquisitions continue to provide the money necessary to successfully find an eventual replacement for tableware.

For some period of time, as stainless imports continued to bite into the domestic market, the upgrading of quality levels has offset the unit decline and thus roughly maintained factory production hours. Now, with the continuing drop in unit sales, it would seem that we must look forward to having to shrink a fine organization whose people and systems are an asset that would be the envy of many manufacturing companies, unless we can find the right kind of long-term work for this organization to do.

Residual Strengths

Tableware has provided us with many possibilities and these account for its longevity. It lends itself to differentiation by trademark, design and quality range while fulfilling a basic human need. It finds its way in increasing quantities into every home in a growing nation as well as into food service and special markets. It offers good gross profit possibilities and high value to cost of shipment, and it adapts easily to display, promotion and advertising. However, in its early days, it had to establish itself against entrenched competition that possessed technology, trained workers, distribution and trade-mark recognition. Accordingly, O. L. tableware losses had to be subsidized by established businesses for some years.

Just as animal traps faced the prospect of diminished overseas markets and the raising of fur-bearing animals and just as the canning business presented the necessity to produce and preserve on a national basis, so now the tableware business confronts us with seemingly inexorable unit-volume declines as importers of long-standing are joined by former domestic manufacturers who increasingly import low cost, good quality product from the Far East under their own names. This process will gradually force us to shift more domestic production overseas with resultant impact on volume variances and overhead structure, unless a family of new products is once found to take up the slack.

The tableware business provides us with various strengths around which to focus our efforts in this direction:

- a respected name well known to all constituencies (consumer, trade, financial);
- well maintained, modern facilities;
- educated, trained, motivated people at all levels;

- an effective, comprehensive and tested management structure;
- technology applicable to metal manufacturing; and
- an established distribution network.

An Approach to the Answer

Discussing and deciding upon the eventual long-term product/market answer to the above problem would seem to require a coordinated but multi-faceted approach. Depending upon what the eventual answer may turn out to be will determine whether it becomes a part of the present OSD operation or whether it is set up as a separate operation using people and facilities acquired from OSD. And, it is possible that the new operation, based in Sherrill, might head up to one of our other subsidiaries.

In any case, time, patience and resources (human and financial) will be needed to find this answer(s), unlike the limited and inconsistent diversification efforts of the past.

For a start, broad criteria should be established to give focus to the search. Among such are:

- market(s), including size, growth, competition, etc.
- product, including type, technology, trademark, etc
- management (if an acquisition), including capability, durability, etc.
- competition, including who, where, can we meet and beat it, why, etc. and
- profitability, including cost, risk, and return.

There are various ways of going about solving our problem and we should undertake and stay with a number of them.

- Investment Bankers and Finders. With our criteria in mind, they may well be able to find companies that would fit our needs and whose operations could be relocated here.
- Universities and Research Centers. I don't know much about the possibilities of this approach except for what I read. These places harbor people with existing new product ideas and/or people to whom one can turn for new ideas to use existing technology.

- In-house R & D. I believe OSD is presently trying to organize this function and may, in time, come up with an in-house solution. Also, it is possible that our stainless flatware can be sufficiently differentiated to offset the built-in cost disadvantage.
- Corporate Market Research. At this point, it would seem as though we need someone at the corporate level to guide overall market research, especially in view of the absence of any formal market research capability in two of our subsidiaries. Such a person would monitor markets we are presently in as well as markets for which we might qualify, maintain a data base and surveillance of emerging trends, and assist divisions or subsidiaries with specific projects as needed.
- Own Search. Corporate and subsidiary personnel can be briefed as to the corporate need and criteria in order that they, in the course of their regular affairs, may discover possibilities for further follow-up and consideration.
- Advertisement. Various quality journals routinely carry advertisements for companies wishing to buy and/or sell products or businesses.
- Friends in the Trade (suppliers and customers). It may be possible to use such of these people, whose discretion and judgment we trust, to keep an eye out for us. Also, they could be selectively interviewed to see who they may know that fit our criteria.

There are undoubtedly other resources that don't occur to me now. Regardless, we have at our disposal a number of avenues we can travel simultaneously. What we need, above all, is a coordinated, consistent commitment to get started and stay the course until we come up with what is needed to see this company, and its community and its values into the 21st century and beyond. And, once started, this process may remain as much an everyday part of corporate life as, say, finance, personnel or any other department.

Appendix 2
Company Parts

What follows are brief sketches of enterprises purchased by Oneida Ltd. in the 1970s to the 1980s.

A. The Tableware Trio

1. <u>Oneida Canada Ltd.</u> Based on the Niagara Falls, Canada site where John Humphrey Noyes lived at the Oneida Community's breakup, this company was protected by tariffs from 1916 until NAFTA came along in 1994. After that, lower-priced imports ruined this business which heretofore had made excellent profits.
2. <u>Oneida Mexicana S. A. (OMSA).</u> This affiliate began as a joint venture in 1968 in Toluca, Mexico. Oneida looked after the manufacturing and its partner, H. Steele Inc., handled marketing. Later, Oneida took over the latter also. The company and its assets were sold in 2008.
3. <u>Oneida Silversmiths Ltd. (OSL).</u> Starting with a small Sheffield factory in the late 1920s, a modern, integrated factory was built in the late 1950s in Northern Ireland. Unfortunately, this company was decimated by cheaper imports and bad management in the early 1970s. The factory was closed in the 1980s and OSL went to selling imported dinnerware.

B. Big and Promising

1. <u>Camden Wire.</u> Purchased in 1976, this excellent company provided diversification into manufacturing industrial copper wire and also excellent sales and profits. Its profits declined in the 1980s due to sustained lower prices for copper, lesser management skills,

venturing into finished wire, and possibly price cutting. It was sold at a modest profit in 1997 and the money used to pay for a dish importer.
2. <u>Buffalo China.</u> This producer of heavy-duty dinnerware was purchased by Oneida in 1983. It had been carefully managed by its owner and ran a very efficient and profitable factory. Oneida upgraded its factory equipment and warehousing while lowering its profits. The factory went from black to red and the place was sold to employees in 2004 at a friendly price.
3. <u>Rena Ware.</u> This was a direct seller to the public, largely in Latin America, of stainless steel cookware and a long-time user of exclusive Oneida flatware as order-closer. Oneida bought the company in 1978. For a couple of years business was good and everyone was happy. When sales fell off and losses cropped up, the opposite was true and Oneida sold Rena Ware back to its original owner at a considerable loss.

C. Small and Incidental

1. <u>Leavens Manufacturing Co.</u> Oneida bought the Attleboro, Massachusetts-based producer of emblematic jewelry in 1973 and recovered about a third of its purchase price from its balance sheet in cash and from sale of its accumulated gold emblems of one kind or another. It was sold in 1986 for a profit of over double its official purchase price.
2. <u>Old Hall.</u> A U.K. producer of stainless steel holloware and flatware was had in 1983 along with a small crystal glass blower. After a few years, Oneida retained only a flatware pattern from this outfit.
3. <u>Webster-Wilcox.</u> This was a famous silverplated holloware trademark of the International Silver Company, Oneida's ancient rival. Oneida overpaid for its name, tools and dies and never produced much of it. Among other things the dies and tools were worn and not compatible with Oneida's machinery.

D. The "Goodwill" Gang

1. <u>Viners.</u> By Sheffield standards, Viners was a newcomer. However, it competed vigorously with Oneida in the early 1960s. It went broke a couple of times in the late 20th century and emerged as a tableware importer of goods from Southeast Asia. It was purchased on June 9, 2001, by Oneida. Price: $25,000,000.
2. <u>Sakura.</u> This was an importer of weird-looking china made, again, in Asia. Oneida bought it for $40,000,000 on June 23, 2001. It lost half its sales when a major customer decided to buy direct.
3. <u>Delco.</u> When all was said and done, Delco cost Oneida about $78,000,000. As was the case for Sakura, Delco lost over 75% of its pre-Oneida sales to the defection of a major customer, lost airline business and an abandoned factory store.

Summary: In 2001, within a three-month period, Oneida spent a total of $143 million in cash for the above three companies of which $114 million (80%) was represented by "goodwill". I was not permitted to see the financial statements—balance sheets, income statements, cash flow statements, that would have supported (or not) the prices paid for the above companies.

Appendix 3
Money Spent vs. Money Earned

Here is a partial list showing, from 1996 onwards, how Oneida Ltd. spent money earned and, later, money largely borrowed.

1996	Rego China Purchase	$46.6 million ($33.8 goodwill)
	Discontinued Operations	$6.8 million
	Camden Wire Sold	$59 million ($3.5 profit)
1997	Australian Acquisitions*	$5 million (guess)
	Schott Crystal	$9 million (minority interest)
	Stock Buy-back	$12.7 million
1998	TTEID (Italy) Purchase	$13 million
	Hotel Glassware Imports	$30 million (estimates vary)
	Consumer Dinnerware**	$5 million
	Restructuring Payments	$4.9 million
1999	Canada Closing	$10.5 million
	Italian Factory Closing	$?
	Buffalo Warehouse Constructed	$11 million
	Libbey Lawsuit, etc.	$18 million
2000	Distribution Center Constructed	$6 million
	Viners Purchase	$25 million
	Sakura Purchase	$40 million
	Delco Purchase Integration	<u>$78 million (all-in)</u>
		$315.5 million Net Total

Here is what was earned over these years:

FY 1997-2001	Profit Before Tax	$171.5 million
FY 1997-2001	Profit After Tax	$69.6 million

Appendix 4
Corporate Financial Highlights by President

A lot of financial statistics have been boiled down in various categories. What follows is some basic information to keep in mind as Oneida Ltd. prospered, declined and then perished.

<u>Corporate Financial Highlights.</u> Shown below are some summary financial results for corporate sales and profits at term-ends of the four final pre-bankrupt Oneida Ltd. presidents.

FY	President	Net Sales	Net Income %	EPShare
1981	P. T. Noyes	$359.6	6.3	$3.22
1986	Marcellus	$252.1	0.07	$0.27
2000	Matthews	$495.0	1.1	$0.33
2004	Kallet	$453.0	(99.37)	($5.98)
2005	Kallet	$415.0	(51.3)	($1.68)

Appendix 5
Special Benefits and Contracts

Special Benefits. The Board of Directors in 2002 provided "Special Benefits" to certain, highly paid executives upon their reaching retirement age. Monthly and yearly retirement payments (Board Amendment date, December 11, 2002) were as follows:

	Month	Full Year
D. DeBarr (Factory)	$7,600	$92,168
T. Fetzner (Finances)	$7,801	$93,616
R. Houle (Personnel)	$9,655	$115,863
P. Kallet (President)	$25,096	$301,163

Then, on April 1, 2004, another board-approved amendment was passed for

A. Conseur (V.P.)	$20,529	$246,348
Total	$70,681	$849,158

May 1, 2004 – Oneida takes a $540,000 first-quarter charge for amending its pension plan to add executive obligations

Employment Contracts. Later, in July 2004, employment contracts were provided for C. Suttmeier, P. Fobare, G. Denny and J. Joseph. Whether these people received any retirement "Special Benefits" is unknown. If not, they may have had to settle for half of their annual salary amount.

Appendix 6
Presidential Salary Growth

Salary Growth vs. Net Income

FY	President	Salary (thousands)	Net Income % to Net Sales
1970	P.T. Noyes	$81	4.0
1975	P.T. Noyes	$78	2.9
1980	P.T. Noyes	$204	5.0
1985	Marcellus	$304	3.6
1990	Matthews	$282	3.6
1995	Matthews	$378	2.7
2000	Kallet	$628	1.1
2003	Kallet	$340	1.9
2005	Kallet	$332	(12.3)

Appendix 7
GNP vs Corporate Profit Graph

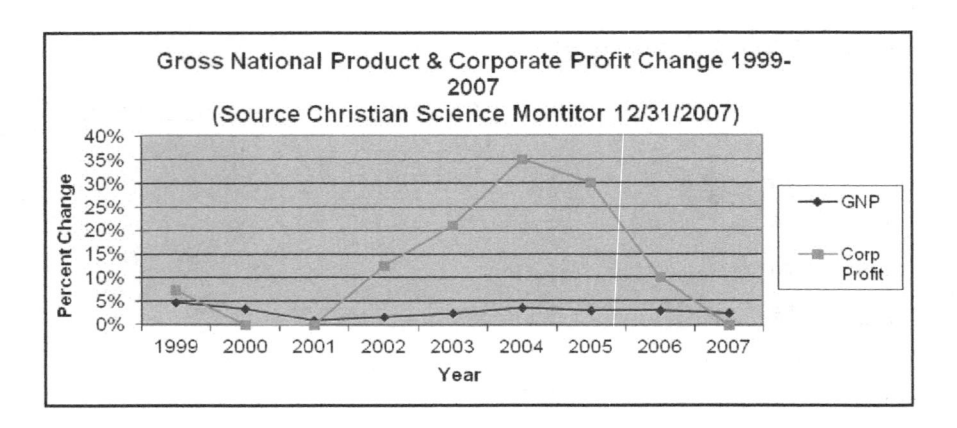

Gross National Product & Corporate Profit Change 1999-2007
(Source Christian Science Montitor 12/31/2007)

The above chart shows overall—movement by year of Gross National Product and overall Corporate profits. Note that profits were not unduly hit by the 9/11 tragedy.

Although Oneida's sales declined slightly from a peak of $516 million in FY 2001 to $480 million in FY 2003, cash flow and income were largely decimated by rapid repayment and a 100% increase in interest payments over the previous three years.

In their joint letter to stockholders in the FY 2000 annual report, Matthews and Kallet ended with these encouraging words: "Oneida's rich heritage, complemented by decisive initiatives that demonstrate our understanding of an evolving marketplace, emphasizes long-term value for our shareholders." As it turned out, the short-term would see loyal shareholders wiped out as unpaid lenders took over and bankruptcy took place

Acknowledgements
"Nota Bevia"

Putting on paper what happened to Oneida Ltd. that led it into bankruptcy in 2006 has taken a lot longer than it should have. The dolorous nature of this unnecessary corporate tragedy promoted a large degree of procrastination while chasing down (or attempting to) the facts of the matter required a considerable amount of time.

I am very mindful of both friends and former OL employees who have encouraged me in this sad task. There are, no doubt, those unhappy that this history of corporate failure should see the light of day.

Had it not been for Tony Wonderley, PhD this book might never have been published. He is a skilled writer of several books and is kept fully busy as the Mansion House Curator. This later situation gave me access to him and as he saw me stumble along on this project he stepped in to offer me invaluable advice and long hours (days?) of his own labor. He effectively edited what I had written; made corrections as indicated, provided extensive footnotes, indexing and even necessary photographs. All that take up this book owe him a debt of gratitude—especially me.

Of special note is the time and effort over many months of my daughter, Elizabeth Hatcher Gayner, who picked her way through my more or less indecipherable handwriting while word processing the text and various revisions to this book. And, she did all this in what little spare time her busy life permits. We share the same birthday and she is truly the best birthday present I ever expect to receive as well as what the Oneida Community would have called "a special providence".

I shall always be grateful to Richard Johnson, formerly Chief of Staff to the Attorney General of Canada and once a marketing executive of Oneida Canada Ltd. Despite his more important responsibilities, Rick offered to edit and index this volume and was a source not only of information but also of encouragement. Special thanks also to others who helped in varying ways with this project. Barry Grabow, former Oneida Ltd. Financial executive who gave suggestions and computer-based information (and also called upon Oneida's board of directors to change top management several years before the company failed). Also, Ed Pitts who once taught philosophy at a large university before taking up the law and marrying an Oneida Community descendent which led him to study her heritage. Ed therefore was able to examine this document on several different levels and angles.

Then, there are various former employees of Oneida Ltd. who made welcome and private contributions of information and advice and in particular my friend and invaluable assistant Marie Magliocca who knew many of the people and things I have written about. She checked the manuscript for accuracy, tone and fairness with her accustomed grace and acuity.

A couple of Oneida Community descendants have put in a lot of time pouring over this document and I am grateful to them. Kathy Garner, PhD, read carefully what was written and provided a number of useful comments and corrections. Then there is Sally Allen Mandel whose family was prominent in the affairs of both the communal beginnings and later the commercial development of Oneida Ltd. In her own right, she is the author of a number of successful novels. She provided a critical examination of this text, helpful questions and suggestions and ongoing encouragement to see it through and get it done. I am very grateful to both of them.

Whatever inaccuracies this record may contain are mine and my fault. What has been written has been done out of a sense of obligation that the accomplishments of Oneida Ltd. be remembered as well as the dreary details of its plunge into bankruptcy and extinction.